500

desserts & sweet treats

500

desserts & sweet treats

the only compendium of desserts you'll ever need

Wendy Sweetser

APPLE

A Quintet Book

First published in the UK in 2012 by
Apple Press
7 Greenland Street
London NW1 0ND
United Kingdom

www.apple-press.com

ISBN: 978-1-84543-448-9
QTT.5DBE

This book was conceived, designed and produced by
Quintet Publishing Limited
6 Blundell Street
London N7 9BH
United Kingdom

Food Stylist: Wendy Sweetser
Photographer: Ria Osborne
Art Director: Michael Charles
Editorial Assistant: Holly Willsher
Editorial Director: Donna Gregory
Publisher: Mark Searle

10 9 8 7 6 5 4 3 2 1

Printed in China by 1010 Printing International Ltd.

contents

introduction

For many of us – whatever our age – the most eagerly anticipated part of a meal is a wickedly indulgent dessert. Whether it's dark and chocolatey, light and frothy or warm and comforting, nothing can quite beat that first spoonful of heavenly sweet delight when a bowl of luscious trifle, mousseor pie is placed in front of us. The word "dessert" comes from the French verb *desservir* meaning to "clear the table," but all dessert lovers will agree that clearing the table is the last thing on their mind when a dessert is about to appear.

Every country has its own favourite way of rounding off a memorable meal. In France, pâtisserie shop windows glisten with jewel-like fruit tarts; in Britain, memories of Sunday lunch at grandma's have created a lifelong fondness for steamed sponges and fruit crumbles; while the indulgent dessert capital of the world – the United States – has introduced the rest of us to light-as-air cheesecakes, melt-in-the-mouth chocolate brownies, ice cream and whoopie pies.

Although desserts as we now know them first became popular in the seventeenth century, serving something sweet had been the favourite way to end a meal long before that. The Romans preserved fruits as sweetmeats; Tudor kings and queens of England enjoyed sugared almonds, jellies and marzipan; while the Frenchman Marie-Antoine Carême became the first celebrity chef when he created elaborately sculptured desserts for the world leaders of the day, including Napoleon and Britain's King George IV.

rocky road cookies, page 207

choux ring with stawberries & blueberries, page 121

With the arrival of the nineteenth century, more and more chefs came up with new ideas and dessert trolleys everywhere began to groan under the weight of increasingly ornate confections. Some desserts were considered so special they were named after favourite celebrities. Peach Melba was created in the early 1890s by Auguste Escoffier, the head chef at the Savoy Hotel in London, for the celebrated Australian soprano Dame Nellie Melba. Another was Pavlova, a cloud of crisp-coated meringue with a soft-as-marshmallow centre, that both Australians and New Zealanders claim the credit for having invented to honor Anna Pavlova, the Russian ballerina, when she visited their shores.

No single book could hope to include a recipe for every dessert that's ever been invented. In the following pages of *500 Desserts*, you'll find lots of your favourites, given a new or unexpected twist. We hope you'll be tempted to try some previously undiscovered treats and be inspired to create new recipes of your own.

plum frangipane tarts, page 95

equipment

Most desserts in this book can be made using basic kitchen equipment, although if you're a keen and adventurous cook you might want to invest in a few extra items.

The basics are: mixing bowls of different sizes; measuring spoons and scales (which are invaluable if you're doing a lot of baking); rolling pin; grater; wooden spoons; hand whisk; wire-mesh sieve; cutting board; small and large chopping knives and serrated knife.

Also, large and small saucepans; baking trays; wire cooling rack; spatula; and finally, waxed paper, aluminum foil, clingfilm and baking parchment.

The extras include:

electric mixer
An electric hand whisk or freestanding food mixer makes light work of all sorts of time-consuming tasks, such as making meringues, whipping cream, whisking custard mixtures, creaming cake batters and beating choux pastry.

food processor & liquidiser
Food processors are useful for grinding dry ingredients such as nuts, biscuits and spices to a powder and also for puréeing fruits. Liquidisers work in a similar way, grinding and puréeing ingredients, but they require at least some liquid to be added to the mixture for them to work efficiently.

baking tins & ovenproof dishes

If you're going to be serious about making desserts, you'll need a variety of baking tins in various shapes and sizes. Loaf tins, round and square cake tins, as well as springform tins, muffin tins and quiche or flan tins are essential for a baker.

Additionally, a few ramekins or other small ovenproof cups or dishes for baking mousses, soufflés and custards are useful for quite a few of the recipes in this book and have many other uses.

serving plates & dishes

A selection of attractive serving plates, bowls, dishes and especially small glass dishes of varying sizes will show off your culinary creations to maximum advantage. These needn't be made from the best china or cut glass – pretty side plates, plain wine glasses, inexpensive glass bowls will all work well. Remember that any dish that needs to go into the oven or under the grill must be heatproof to a high temperature.

white chocolate torte, page 37

cinnamon meringue slice layered with caribbean fruits, page 117

ingredients

Think of all the things you love to eat – ice cream, chocolate, cake, fresh fruit, cream – and you'll find them in desserts. It's what makes them so irresistible!

butter & oil

I prefer unsalted butter rather than salted – and definitely not margarine - for all my baking. Occasionally oils are used and my preference is sunflower oil because it's mild-flavoured. It's also ideal when a tin needs to be greased.

chocolate

Choose good-quality chocolate whether you're buying plain, milk or white. Plain chocolate that contains a high percentage of cocoa solids (above 70%) is generally too intensely flavoured for desserts – 50-60% being preferable. The flavour of plain chocolate desserts will mellow if the dessert is prepared the day before.
Milk chocolate should contain at least 30% cocoa solids. For cocoa powder, use pure unsweetened cocoa to give an intense chocolate flavour.

eggs

Although large eggs are used in the majority of recipes in this book, size is not crucial in most instances and medium eggs can be substituted if that's all you have available.

One exception is choux pastry, where medium-size eggs are the right size to give the soft texture needed for choux paste while ensuring the mixture still holds its shape. If too much egg is added, the paste will spread when it bakes in the oven and you'll end up with flat, doughy profiteroles rather than crisp, round golf balls.

essences
When buying essences, such as vanilla, peppermint and almond, buy good-quality ones, which will make a real difference in the taste of the finished dish. Use them sparingly, as they are very strong.

flour & sugar
Use the flour called for in a recipe. I like self-raising flour for cakes and plain flour for pastries (except when making choux pastry – profiteroles - where white bread flour gives a better result). Cornflour is used for sauces.

For sugar, caster, granulated, light and dark brown and icing are what you'll need.

fruits
For cooking, use fresh fruit when in season; otherwise, use fruit that has been canned in juice rather than syrup. Also, use freshly squeezed citrus juices to get the best flavour.

blueberry muffin trifles, page 142

chocolate brownie gateau, page 212

gelatin

Powdered, unflavoured gelatin needs to be sprinkled over a little cold liquid in a small bowl, left to soak for 5 minutes so the granules swell and then dissolved by standing the bowl in a pan of hot, but not boiling, water. Once completely dissolved, the mix is stirred into the other recipe ingredients. It is essential that the gelatin has fully dissolved; if not, you'll find lumps in your dessert.

reduced-fat products

The full-fat milk, creams, cream cheese and yogurt used in the recipes can be replaced with reduced-fat alternatives in most instances. However, if low-fat products are heated – for example, reduced-fat cream in a sauce – they should not be boiled hard or the sauce will curdle.

salt

Some cooks swear by adding a pinch of salt to every dish, while for health reasons others avoid it altogether. The recipes in this book don't have added salt but if you generally add salt to a recipe, do so; the choice is yours. Alternatively, the unsalted butter used in the recipes can be replaced with salted butter.

brown sugar

During storage, soft brown sugar particles can stick together in clumps and become hard. To make the sugar soft again, tip it into a bowl, cover with a damp cloth and leave overnight or grind the sugar in a food processor to eliminate any lumps.

techniques

Mastering a few simple basic techniques is the key to producing perfect desserts every time.

melting chocolate

If chocolate is melted at too high a temperature, it will develop a white bloom as it cools and resets so care needs to be taken when melting it. To do this, break or chop the bar into small pieces, place in a heatproof bowl and stand the bowl over a pan of gently simmering – not boiling – water, making sure the bottom of the bowl is not in contact with the water. Leave until the chocolate melts, stirring occasionally until smooth. Alternatively, chocolate can be melted in the microwave on defrost setting in 30 second bursts, again stirring until smooth.

working with light sponge & mousse mixes

Before baking a light whisked sponge batter or leaving a mousse to set, tap the container the mixture is in on the work surface to allow any large air bubbles to rise to the surface and burst.

individual raspberry soufflés, page 74

whisking egg whites

The secret to perfect meringues and other dishes containing whisked egg whites is to whisk the whites to soft peaks first before starting to add the sugar. To begin with, add the sugar 1 teaspoonful at a time until the whites start to thicken and become shiny. The remaining sugar can then be added in a steady stream. If sugar is added too quickly, the egg whites will be unable to incorporate it quickly enough, resulting in the whites not whipping up to sufficient bulk and the sugar leaking out as syrup when the meringues dry out in the oven.

To make meringues that are dry and crisp all the way through, place them in the oven on its lowest setting for several hours so the liquid in the egg whites evaporates and the meringues dry out and become crisp. A pavlova is different in that it is "baked" at a slightly higher temperature so the outer shell becomes dry and crisp but the centre is still soft and marshmallowy.

folding in egg whites

When folding in egg whites, it's important to do it gently so all the air you've whisked into the whites isn't beaten out. However, as the mixture you're folding the whites into is likely to be quite heavy, soften it first by stirring in a tablespoonful of the whites. Once incorporated, fold in the remainder of the whites using a large metal spoon and a figure-eight motion.

toasting nuts

Nuts can be toasted under a conventional grill, in a dry frying pan over a low heat or spread out on a baking tray in a low oven. Whichever method you choose, watch the nuts carefully and turn them over from time to time, as they quickly go from golden brown to black and burned.

coffee meringue kisses, page 122

basic recipes

chocolate sauce

For a smooth, luscious chocolate sauce to serve warm or cold, melt 40 grams (1½ ounces) unsalted butter, 200 ml (7 fl oz) double cream and 225 grams (8 ounces) chopped plain chocolate over low heat until the butter and chocolate melt, stirring until smooth.

For a chocolate fudge sauce to serve warm, heat 55 grams (2 ounces) unsalted butter, 55 grams (2 ounces) light brown sugar and 55 grams (2 ounces) chopped plain chocolate gently in a pan until the chocolate melts. Stir in 40 ml (1½ fl oz) double cream until smooth, then simmer for 2-3 minutes.

fruit sauce or coulis

For a simple fruit sauce or coulis, purée 300 grams (11 ounces) of your chosen fruit with 2 tablespoons icing sugar and 1 tablespoon lemon juice until smooth. Raspberry and blackberry coulis can be strained if you want to remove the seeds.

fresh custard

To make thick custard, measure 600 ml (1 pint) milk into a measuring jug and pour all but about 4 tablespoons of it into a saucepan. Mix 6 large egg yolks, 2 teaspoons cornflour and 55 grams (2 ounces) caster sugar with the milk left in the measuring jug until smooth. Bring the milk in the saucepan to the boil, pour into the measuring

thai coconut pancakes with watermelon, star fruit & pomegranate seeds, page 238

jug and whisk with the egg yolk mixture until combined. Pour everything back into the saucepan and stir continuously or whisk over low heat until thick and smooth. If making the custard ahead, dust the surface with a little sugar to prevent a skin forming as it cools.

For a thinner custard, increase the quantity of milk to 750 ml (1¼ pints). For a richer custard, replace half the milk with single cream. The custard can be flavoured with vanilla, almond, coffee, grated orange or lemon rind or 1 teaspoon unflavoured cocoa powder, mixed with the egg yolks.

brown bread & hazelnut ice cream, page 178

ultimate chocolate desserts

When it comes to indulgence, there's really nothing better than chocolate, whether it's a dark and sumptuous mousse, a sustaining bread and butter pudding or a light, creamy roulade with a tangy raspberry filling.

chocolate velvet ganache gâteau

see variations page 47

This is equally good served as a dessert or as a special cake to celebrate a birthday or anniversary. Let the ganache cool at room temperature rather than in the fridge.

for the cake
150 ml (4½ fl oz) plain yogurt
150 ml (4½ fl oz) sunflower oil
225 g (8 oz) dark brown sugar
3 large eggs
285 g (10 oz) self-raising flour
1 tsp baking powder
85 g (3 oz) unsweetened cocoa powder
2 tbsp milk

for the ganache & filling
175 ml (6 fl oz) whipping cream
200 g (9 oz) plain chocolate, chopped
2 tbsp apricot jam
chocolate shavings and chocolate truffles,
    to decorate

To make the cake, grease a 20-cm (8-inch) springform tin and line base and sides with baking parchment. Preheat oven to 160°C (325°F/gas mark 3). Place yogurt, oil, sugar and eggs in a mixing bowl. Beat together until smooth and evenly combined. Sieve in flour, baking powder and cocoa, then fold in gently with a large metal spoon. Pour mixture into prepared tin and bake for about 40–45 minutes or until a cocktail stick inserted in the centre comes out clean. Cool in tin for 10 minutes, then turn out onto a wire rack to cool completely. To make the ganache, bring cream to the boil in a small pan. Remove from heat and stir in chocolate until it melts. Beat with a wooden spoon until mixture is smooth, then allow to cool at room temperature until thick enough to spread, stirring occasionally. Whisk for 1–2 minutes until light and creamy. Split cake in half through the centre. Spread bottom layer with apricot jam. Place second layer on top and spread top and sides with chocolate ganache. Decorate with chocolate shavings and truffles. The cake will keep in the refrigerator for several days.

Serves 12

molten chocolate cakes

see variations page 48

A classic chocolate dessert that's rich, dark and oh so satisfying. It's important to serve the puddings as soon as they come out of the oven so the soft gooey centres don't overcook and become dry.

canola oil, for greasing
175 g (6 oz) plain chocolate, chopped
125 ml (4 fl oz) whipping cream
3 large eggs

3 tbsp dark brown sugar
½ tsp vanilla essence
1 tbsp plain flour

Preheat oven to 220°C (425°F/gas mark 7). Grease four mini pudding basins or ramekins with a little rapeseed oil and line the bases with a round of baking parchment. Put chocolate and cream in a large bowl and place the bowl over a pan of simmering water. Leave until chocolate has melted, then stir until smooth. In another bowl, beat eggs, sugar, vanilla and flour together until evenly mixed.

Gradually beat in the (still warm) melted chocolate. Spoon or pour mixture into prepared basins or ramekins and set them on a baking tray. Bake for 10 minutes or until set on the outside but still quite soft in the centre. Turn puddings out onto serving plates, dust with cocoa powder and serve at once.

Serves 4

white & dark zebra creams

see variations page 49

An eye-catching variation on traditional chocolate mousse. Use good-quality plain chocolate but not one with a high percentage of cocoa solids or the flavour will be too bitter.

110 ml (4 fl oz) full-fat soured cream
250 ml (8 fl oz) double cream
55 g (2 oz) white chocolate, chopped
175 g (6 oz) plain chocolate, chopped

2 egg whites
2 tbsp light brown sugar
grated dark and white chocolate and chocolate
    curls, to decorate

Heat soured cream and double cream together in a pan until they just come to the boil. Pour about one-third of the hot mixture into a bowl and stir in white chocolate until melted. Stir plain chocolateinto the larger quantity of hot cream until melted. Leave both to cool.

Whisk egg whites until soft peak stage and then gradually whisk in sugar until stiff. Fold about one-third of the whites into the white chocolate mixture and the rest into the dark.

Spoon half the plain chocolate mixture into 4 glass dessert dishes or tumblers and chill for about 30 minutes until just set. Spoon the white chocolate mixture on top and return to the refrigerator for another 30 minutes or until just set. Spoon the remaining plain chocolate mixture on top and chill for 1 hour or until ready to serve. To serve, decorate with grated dark and white chocolate and chocolate curls.

Serves 4

bitter chocolate tart with toasted hazelnut crust

see variations page 50

This is a deliciously smooth, plain chocolate tart that can be served warm or cold.

for the pastry
25 g (1 oz) finely ground toasted hazelnuts
175 g (6 oz) plain flour
85 g (3 oz) unsalted butter, cut into
   small pieces
1 tbsp icing sugar
1 large egg yolk
about 1 tbsp cold water

for the filling
200 g (7 oz) dark chocolate, chopped
150 g (4½ oz) unsalted butter
2 large eggs
2 large egg yolks
55 g (2 oz) dark brown sugar
55 g (2 oz) cocoa powder
125 ml (4 fl oz) hot water
25 g (1 oz) chopped toasted hazelnuts

In a food processor, blend hazelnuts, flour and butter until mixture resembles breadcrumbs. Add icing sugar, egg yolk and water. Blend until dough comes together in a ball. Wrap in clingfilm and chill for 30 minutes. Preheat oven to 200°C (400°F/gas mark 6). Roll out pastry on a floured surface and use it to line a 28x18-cm (7x11-inch) flan tin. Line pastry with waxed paper, fill with baking beans and bake for 20 minutes, removing beans and paper after 15 minutes. Remove tin from oven and reduce temperature to 150°C (300°F/gas mark 2). To make the filling, melt chocolate and butter in the microwave on low for about 5 minutes. Stir until smooth. In another bowl, beat eggs, egg yolks and brown sugar. Fold into melted mixture. Whisk cocoa powder in hot water, then fold into chocolate mixture until combined. Pour filling into crust and bake for 10–15 minutes or until filling is just set. Serve topped with chopped toasted hazelnuts.
Serves 8-10

white chocolate torte

see variations page 51

Make this deliciously smooth and creamy cake in a tin with a removable base, as the finished dessert will be much easier to remove.

for the sponge base
175 g (6 oz) unsalted butter
175 g (6 oz) caster sugar
3 large eggs, beaten
150 g (5½ oz) self-raising flour
25 g (1 oz) unsweetened cocoa powder
for the mousse
1½ tbsp unflavoured gelatin
350 ml (12 fl oz) milk

65 g (2½ oz) cornflour
100 g (3½ oz) caster sugar
225 g (8 oz) white chocolate, chopped
2 tbsp white rum
350 ml (12 fl oz) double cream
to decorate
extra whipped cream
chocolate malt sweets

Grease a 20x30-cm (8x12-inch) cake tin and line with baking parchment. Preheat oven to 190°C (375°F/gas mark 5). Beat butter and sugar until creamy. Gradually beat in eggs. Sieve and fold in flour and cocoa. Spoon mixture into tin, smooth and bake for 20 minutes. Turn out, peel off lining paper and allow to cool on a wire rack. With a sharp serrated knife, cut horizontally through the sponge to make two layers. Wash pan, grease and line again with baking parchment so paper comes slightly above sides. Place one sponge layer in tin. To make the mousse, soak gelatin in rum for 5 minutes, then stand bowl in a pan of hot water while you continue with the mousse. Whisk 125 ml (4 fl oz) of the milk with cornflour. Heat remaining milk with the sugar until dissolved and stir this onto cornflour mixture. Return to pan and stir over medium heat until thickened and smooth. Remove pan from heat and stir in chocolate until melted. Fold in gelatin and stir until smooth. Whip cream until it just holds its shape, fold into mousse and pour over sponge base. Place second layer on top, chill until set, then decorate with whipped cream and sweets to serve.

Serves 10-12

chocolate bread & butter pudding

see variations page 52

This dessert is a good way to use up bread that has started to go stale. White or whole wheat bread work equally well. Serve plain or dusted with icing sugar, with custard (pages 24–25) or cream.

10 slices bread
150 g (5½ oz) plain chocolate, chopped
85 g (3 oz) unsalted butter, cut up
250 ml (8 fl oz) whipping cream

200 ml (7 fl oz) reduced-fat crème fraîche
4 tbsp orange juice
110 g (4 oz) light brown sugar
3 large eggs

Cut crusts off bread and cut each slice into 4 triangles. Put chocolate, butter, cream, crème fraîche, orange juice and sugar in a bowl. Microwave on low power for 7–8 minutes or place the bowl over a pan of simmering water until chocolate and butter melt. Stir until smooth. Beat eggs together in a large measuring jug, add melted mixture and whisk until combined. Pour a 1-cm (half-inch) layer into a 20-cm (8-inch) square or 25x30-cm (9x12-inch) ovenproof dish measuring about 6 cm (2½ inches) deep. Arrange half the bread on top, overlapping the triangles. Pour half the remaining chocolate mixture over bread and arrange remaining triangles on top. Cover with remaining mixture, pressing bread down lightly. Cover dish with clingfilm and leave in a cool place or the refrigerator for 4–5 hours. Preheat oven to 180°C (350°F/gas mark 4) and remove clingfilm. Bake pudding for 30–35 minutes or until the top layer of bread is crisp and the chocolate mixture is set. Serve warm.

Serves 6

rich chocolate pots with coffee cream

see variations page 53

Chocolate and coffee are natural partners and combine together beautifully in this classic French dessert. Once the egg yolks have been added, transfer the mixture to a measuring jug to make it easier to pour into the ramekins.

for the chocolate pots
250 ml (8 fl oz) single cream
175 g (6 oz) plain chocolate, chopped
1 tbsp dark brown sugar
4 large egg yolks

for the coffee cream
1 tsp coffee essence (or 1 tsp instant coffee
    dissolved in 1 tbsp hot water)
125 ml (4 fl oz) double or whipping cream
chocolate-covered coffee beans, to decorate

Preheat oven to 150°C (300°F/gas mark 2). To make the chocolate pots, heat cream and chocolate gently together in a pan until chocolate melts. Stir until smooth, then remove pan from heat and whisk in sugar and egg yolks, one at a time. Strain mixture into 4 ramekins or similar small dishes. Place them in a roasting tin. Pour enough hot, but not boiling, water into the pan to come two-thirds up the sides of the dishes. Cover pan with foil. Bake for 30 minutes or until just set. Remove, allow to cool, then chill for 1 hour or longer before serving.

To make the coffee cream, whisk coffee essence and cream together until it just holds its shape. Spoon or pipe the cream on top of the chocolate pots and decorate with chocolate coffee beans.

Serves 4

chocolate waves with dark chocolate mousse

see variations page 54

A chocolate mille-feuille that, instead of layers of puff pastry, uses fine waves of marbled chocolate to sandwich the rich and creamy mousse.

for the waves
175 g (6 oz) plain chocolate, chopped
55 g (2 oz) white chocolate, chopped

for the mousse
150 g (5½ oz) plain chocolate, chopped
3 large eggs, separated
125 ml (4 fl oz) double cream

To make the waves, melt plain chocolate in a bowl over a pan of steaming water. Melt white chocolate in a separate bowl in the same way. Allow both to cool. Cut 8 pieces of baking parchment about 12x10 cm (5x4 inches). Lay chopsticks, wooden spoon handles or pencils on a board, taping in place if necessary. the plain chocolate over the parchment to about 1 cm (½ inch) from the edges and while still wet, spoon the white chocolate into a small paper piping bag and pipe fine lines back and forth across the dark chocolate. Pull the tip of a cocktail stick through the white chocolate lines to make a feathered pattern. Lay parchment pieces over chopsticks so the chocolate sets in waves. When set, carefully peel away the parchment. To make the mousse, melt chocolate until smooth and beat in egg yolks, one at a time. In another bowl, whip cream until it just holds its shape, then fold it into the melted chocolate. Whisk egg whites until they reach soft peaks and fold into chocolate mixture. Transfer mousse to a bowl and chill for several hours. Place a chocolate wave on each serving plate and top with scoops of chocolate mousse and the remaining chocolate waves.

Serves 4

steamed chocolate sponge with vanilla custard

see variations page 55

For a warming winter pudding, nothing will beat these feel-good sponges.

for the sponges
110 g (4 oz) unsalted butter, cut up
125 g (4½ oz) plain chocolate, chopped
3 large eggs
110 g (4 oz) light brown sugar
85 g (3 oz) plain flour
25 g (1 oz) unsweetened cocoa powder, plus
    extra to dust

for the custard
250 ml (8 fl oz) milk
125 ml (4 fl oz) double cream
1 vanilla pod
1 tbsp cornflour
2–3 tbsp caster sugar (according to
    personal taste)
1 large whole egg and 1 large egg yolk, beaten

For the sponges, melt the butter and chocolate together in a bowl set over a pan of simmering water. Stir until smooth, remove and cool. Grease four 200-ml (7-fl oz) pudding basins or ramekins with oil and base line with parchment. Using an electric whisk, beat eggs and sugar until thick and creamy, about 10 minutes. Sieve in flour and cocoa powder and fold in to combine. Pour in chocolate mixture and gently fold in. Spoon mixture into prepared dishes and cover with foil. Steam in a covered basket or colander over boiling water for 45 minutes or until sponges feel firm. To make the custard, blend 4 tablespoons of the milk with the cornflour. Pour remaining milk and cream into a pan. Split vanilla pod lengthwise and scrape seeds into the pan. Bring almost to the boil, then pour onto cornflour mixture, stirring constantly. Return mixture to pan over medium heat and stir until thickened. Whisk in sugar and beaten egg and strain into a serving jug. Turn out sponges on serving plates and peel off paper. Serve hot, dusted with cocoa powder, topped with custard.

Serves 4

chocolate almond tuile baskets with chocolate-dipped strawberries

see variations page 56

The tuile recipe will make more than you need, so store the extras to serve with coffee.

for the tuile baskets
85 g (3 oz) unsalted butter
110 g (4 oz) caster sugar
2 egg whites
85 g (2 oz) plain flour
1 tsp unsweetened cocoa powder
2 tbsp toasted flaked almonds

for the strawberries & cream
85 g (3 oz) white chocolate
16 large or 24 small whole strawberries
110 g (4 oz) milk chocolate, chopped
250 ml (8 fl oz) double cream
chocolate shavings, to decorate

Line two baking trays with baking parchment and draw two 13-cm (5-inch) circles on each. Preheat oven to 180°C (350°F/gas mark 4). To make the tuile baskets, beat butter and sugar together until creamy. Beat in the egg whites, adding ⅓ at a time with a little of the flour. Fold in rest of flour with the cocoa. Finally stir in the almonds. Spoon 2 teaspoons of the mixture onto each marked circle and spread it out in a thin layer with a palette knife. Bake one tray at a time for 5-6 minutes. Immediately lift tuiles off tin, peel off parchment and shape each into a basket using a small bowl as a mould. Continue with remaining mixture to make about 16 tuiles. To make the filling, melt white chocolate and dip strawberries in until half-coated. Put on a plate lined with foil and leave to set – not in the fridge. In another bowl, melt milk chocolate with the cream, stirring until smooth. Leave in a cool place until the chocolate cream can hold its shape. Spoon mixture into baskets, top with strawberries and decorate with chocolate shavings.

Serves 8

chocolate roulade with chocolate cream & raspberries

see variations page 57

Roulades make impressive and popular desserts and are ideal for parties because they can be made ahead and need no last-minute attention.

for the roulade
6 large eggs, separated
150 g (5½ oz) granulated sugar
55 g (2 oz) unsweetened cocoa powder, sieved

for the chocolate cream & decoration
175 ml (6 fl oz) full-fat crème fraîche
250 g (9 oz) white chocolate, chopped
1 tsp vanilla essence
175 g (6 oz) fresh raspberries
chocolate shapes and grated white chocolate,
    to decorate

For the roulade, preheat oven to 180°C (350°F/gas mark 4). Grease a 23x33 (9x13-inch) Swiss roll tin and line with baking parchment. In a large bowl, whisk egg yolks and sugar until thick and pale. In another bowl, whisk egg whites to soft peaks. Fold whites into egg yolk mixture with the cocoa. Pour mixture into tin and level. Bake for 20 minutes or until springy to the touch. Cool for 5 minutes in tin. Turn out onto a sheet of baking parchment and peel off lining paper. Roll up with the parchment inside and place on a wire rack to cool. To make chocolate cream, in a pan bring crème fraîche to the boil. Remove from heat, stir in chopped chocolate and leave until melted. Add vanilla and beat with a wooden spoon until smooth. Allow to cool until thickened and then whisk until light and creamy. Unroll roulade, discard paper and spread with one-third of the chocolate cream. Scatter most of the raspberries over the cream, saving a few. Roll up roulade and spread with remaining chocolate cream. Decorate with raspberries, chocolate shapes and white chocolate.
Serves 8

variations

chocolate velvet ganache gâteau

see base recipe page 29

red velvet gâteau
Prepare basic recipe, adding 2 tablespoons red paste food colouring to yogurt
and eggs, making the ganache with white chocolate and replacing apricot jam
with strawberry jam. Decorate top with fresh strawberries.

apricot & chocolate velvet gâteau
Prepare basic recipe, adding chopped fresh apricots between layers.

chocolate box gâteau
Prepare basic recipe, replacing ganache with chocolate buttercream made by
beating together 225 grams (8 ounces) unsalted butter, 200 grams (7 ounces)
sieved icing sugar and 25 grams (1 ounce) cocoa powder. Press chocolate sponge
fingers around sides of gateau and top with chocolates.

chocolate & brandy truffle gâteau
For adults, prepare basic recipe, pricking cake layers with a skewer and spooning
brandy or Amaretto Disaronno liqueur over them before sandwiching with
apricot jam. Decorate with chocolate brandy truffles.

chocolate & blueberry cream gâteau
Prepare basic recipe, replacing apricot jam with whipped cream and blueberry
jam. Spread top with whipped cream and scatter blueberries on top.

variations

molten chocolate cakes

see base recipe page 30

molten chocolate & yogurt puddings
For a less rich flavour, prepare basic recipe, replacing whipping cream with
crème fraîche or Greek yogurt. Serve with fruit compote.

molten mocha puddings
Prepare basic recipe, replacing vanilla essence with 1 teaspoon coffee
flavouring and adding 2 tablespoons coffee liqueur to chocolate mixture.

molten chocolate & orange puddings
Prepare basic recipe, replacing vanilla essence with grated rind of 1 orange.
Scatter over 2 tablespoons finely chopped pistachios.

molten chocolate & chilli puddings
Prepare basic recipe, omitting vanilla essence and adding 1 seeded and very
finely chopped red chilli. More or less chilli can be added according to
personal taste, but, remember, the smaller the chilli, the hotter it usually is!

molten chocolate & marshmallow puddings
Prepare basic recipe, Press a marshmallow into the centre of each one,
making sure they are completely immersed in the chocolate mixture,
before baking.

white & dark zebra creams

see base recipe page 33

minty zebra creams
Prepare basic recipe, stirring 1 teaspoon finely chopped fresh mint into the dark chocolate.

zebra cream swirls
Prepare basic recipe, dividing hot creams equally between two bowls and stirring 85 grams (3 ounces) plain chocolate into one and 85 grams (3 ounces) white chocolate into the other. Add in alternate spoonfuls to the glasses and swirl with a skewer.

zebra creams with toasted pecans
Prepare basic recipe, sprinkling a thin layer of chopped toasted pecans between each layer and topping with more chopped nuts.

zigzag zebra creams
Prepare basic recipe. Place several food cans on their side in the refrigerator. Holding each glass at an angle, spoon in half the dark mixture and then prop against the cans. Leave until starting to set, then holding glasses on opposite angle, spoon in white mixture. Set again, add remaining dark mixture on top and stand glasses upright.

orange zebra creams
Prepare basic recipe, adding grated rind of 1 orange to dark chocolate.

variations

bitter chocolate tart with toasted hazelnut crust

see base recipe page 34

bitter chocolate & ginger tart with cinnamon crust
Prepare basic recipe, omitting hazelnuts in the pastry and adding 55 g (2 oz) plain flour and 1 teaspoon ground cinnamon to the pastry. Stir 1 tablespoon finely chopped preserved stem ginger into melted chocolate and butter when making the filling.

bitter chocolate tart with chocolate crust
Prepare basic recipe, replacing 1 tablespoon flour in pastry with cocoa.

mocha tart with hazelnut crust
Prepare basic recipe, serving the tart cold, topped with whipped cream flavoured with coffee essence, Tia Maria, Kahlúa or brandy. Sprinkle toasted hazelnuts on top.

bitter chocolate tart with crumb crust
Prepare basic recipe, replacing pastry with a digestive biscuit or chocolate crumb crust. Chill while preparing filling and omit baking blind.

bitter chocolate tarts with walnut crust
Prepare basic recipe, replacing toasted ground hazelnuts in pastry with walnuts and hazelnuts on top with walnuts.

white chocolate torte

see base recipe page 37

white chocolate & almond torte
Prepare basic recipe, replacing cocoa powder in sponge base with
ground almonds.

milk chocolate torte
Prepare basic recipe, replacing white chocolate in the mousse with good-quality
milk chocolate and replacing rum with Irish cream liqueur or orange juice.

white chocolate torte with a crumb crust
Prepare basic recipe, replacing sponge base with your favourite biscuit crumb
crust. Press ²/₃ of the crumbs over bottom of pan, chill for 30 minutes and then
pour mousse mixture on top. When set, gently press rest of crumbs on top.

white chocolate & strawberry torte
Prepare basic recipe, replacing half of cream in the filling with 8 large
strawberries puréed with 2 tablespoons orange juice. Whip remaining cream
until just holding its shape, then fold in strawberry purée.

plain chocolate torte
Prepare basic recipe, replacing white chocolate in mousse with plain chocolate
and the plain chocolate for decoration with white chocolate.

variations

chocolate bread & butter pudding

see base recipe page 38

chocolate brioche pudding
Prepare basic recipe, replacing the bread with slices of brioche or panettone.

chocolate bread & butter pudding with dried fruits
Prepare basic recipe, scattering 110 grams (4 ounces) chopped stoned prunes, dried cranberries or a mixture of the two, over the first layer of bread triangles before pouring in remaining cream mixture and topping with remaining bread.

chocolate & pear bread & butter pudding
Prepare basic recipe, scattering 2 chopped pear halves (canned or fresh) over the first layer of bread triangles before pouring in remaining cream mixture and adding remaining bread.

nutty chocolate bread & butter pudding
Prepare basic recipe, sprinkling 55 grams (2 ounces) chopped walnuts or pecans on top before baking.

orange, banana & chocolate bread & butter pudding
Prepare basic recipe, arranging 1 sliced banana and segments of 1 orange over the first layer of bread triangles before pouring in remaining cream mixture and adding remaining bread.

rich chocolate pots with coffee cream

see base recipe page 41

double chocolate pots with coffee cream
Prepare basic recipe for chocolate pots, heating half the single cream with
85 grams (3 ounces) plain chocolate and the other half with 3 ounces white
chocolate. Add alternating spoonfuls of chocolate mixtures to ramekins and swirl
before baking.

rich chocolate pots with chocolate cream
Prepare basic recipe for the coffee cream, replacing coffee essence with
2 teaspoons unsweetened cocoa powder dissolved in 1 tablespoon hot water.

rich chocolate & cherry pots
Prepare basic recipe for chocolate pots, using larger ramekins and placing
4 or 5 stoned cherries, raspberries or banana slices in the base of each before
adding chocolate mixture. Top with coffee cream or plain cream.

rich chocolate & coconut pots
Prepare basic recipe for chocolate pots, replacing half the single cream with
coconut milk. Instead of coffee, flavour the cream with a few drops of coconut
flavouring . Decorate with a sprinkling of toasted flaked coconut.

rich milk chocolate pots
Prepare basic recipe for chocolate pots, replacing plain chocolate with good-
quality milk chocolate and omitting the brown sugar.

variations

chocolate waves with plain chocolate mousse

see base recipe page 42

mousse-filled brandy snaps
Prepare basic recipe, replacing chocolate waves with brandy snaps.

white chocolate mousse waves
Prepare basic recipe, using white chocolate and 1 teaspoon vanilla essence.

chocolate mousse & strawberry stacks
Prepare basic recipe, spooning plain chocolate onto twelve 1-cm (½-inch) circles drawn on parchment, feathering with white chocolate and laying flat to set. Sandwich in layers with mousse and sliced strawberries.

mousse-filled chocolate baskets
Prepare basic recipe, spooning plain chocolateonto four 15-cm (6-inch) circles drawn on parchment. Feather with white chocolate, lift into shallow bowls and let set. Peel off parchment and fill "baskets" with mousse and fresh fruits.

mousse-filled chocolate & almond waves
Prepare basic recipe, sprinkling plain chocolate with chopped almonds.

steamed chocolate sponge with vanilla custard

see base recipe page 44

steamed chocolate & raisin sponges with vanilla bean custard
Prepare basic sponge recipe, folding in 110 grams (4 ounces) raisins with melted chocolate.

steamed chocolate sponges with chocolate custard
Prepare basic custard recipe, beating 25 grams (1 ounce) cocoa powder with egg.

steamed chocolate chip sponges with vanilla bean custard
Prepare basic sponge recipe, omitting plain chocolate and melting the butter on its own. Fold in 125 grams (4½ ounces) plain chocolate chips with flour and cocoa powder.

steamed chocolate & pecan sponges with vanilla bean custard
Prepare basic sponge recipe, folding 85 grams (3 ounces) chopped pecans into chocolate.

steamed chocolate & ginger sponges with ginger custard
Prepare basic sponge recipe, folding in 1 tablespoon finely chopped preserved stem ginger with the melted chocolate. For the custard, omit vanilla and replace sugar with 2–3 tablespoons syrup from the ginger jar.

variations

chocolate almond tuile baskets with chocolate-dipped strawberries

see base recipe page 45

nutty chocolate baskets with strawberries & cream
Prepare basic recipe for tuile baskets, replacing almonds with toasted chopped hazelnuts, pecansor walnuts.

chocolate & glacé fruit baskets with strawberries & cream
Prepare basic recipe for tuile baskets, replacing half the almonds with finely chopped glacé fruits such as cherries, pineapple or citrus peel.

chocolate tuile baskets with chocolate-dipped fruits
Prepare basic recipe, replacing strawberries with other fresh fruits (such as seedless grapes, kumquats, cherries on stalks and/or pineapple pieces blotted dry with kitchen paper), dipped halfway in white, dark or milk chocolate.

chocolate tuile baskets with strawberries & plain chocolate cream
Prepare basic recipe, replacing white chocolate in the cream with dark or good-quality milk chocolate.

chocolate tuile baskets with strawberries & ice cream
Prepare basic recipe, replacing white chocolate cream with scoops of ice cream.

chocolate roulade with chocolate cream & raspberries

see base recipe page 46

chocolate roulade with strawberries & almonds

Prepare basic recipe, scattering roulade with 2 tablespoons flaked almonds before baking. Make half the white chocolate cream and use to fill roulade, substituting strawberries for raspberries. Omit cream covering. Dust with icing sugar.

festive chocolate roulade

Prepare basic recipe, making the chocolate cream with plain chocolate and replacing raspberries with 110 grams (4 ounces) fresh cranberries simmered with a little sugar until they "pop". Decorate roulade with holly leaves and berries made of coloured marzipan or sugarpaste.

chocolate roulade with mixed berries

Prepare basic recipe, replacing raspberries with mixed berries and currants.

chocolate roulade with raspberries & milk chocolate cream

Prepare basic recipe, replacing white chocolate with good-quality milk chocolate.

chocolate roulade with apricots & cream

Prepare basic recipe, replacing chocolate cream with 250 ml (8 fl oz) cream, whipped. Chop 5 apricots and fold into two-thirds of the cream. Use to fill the roulade. Cover with remaining cream and decorate with apricots.

cheesecakes, sponges & hot soufflés

Creamy cheesecakes to linger over, sticky sponges

to keep out the winter chill and hot puffy soufflés

that must be eaten straight from the oven. This

chapter has something for every occasion,

whether it's a formal dinner or a lunch with

family and friends.

citrus cheesecake with ginger crumb crust

see variations page 75

The easiest way to serve this creamy cheesecake is to cut it into slices with a sharp, serrated knife so the orange slices on top are separated into neat portions.

for the crust
200 g (7 oz) gingersnap biscuits
85 g (3 oz) unsalted butter, melted
1 tsp ground cinnamon
for the cheesecake
finely grated rind and juice of 2 lemons
1½ tbsp unflavoured gelatin
350 g (12 oz) ricotta cheese

250 ml (8 fl oz) Greek yogurt
110 g (4 oz) caster sugar
2 large egg whites
for the topping
2 small oranges, peeled and thinly sliced
1 tsp unflavoured gelatin
125 ml (4 fl oz) freshly squeezed orange juice

To make the crust, grease a 20-cm (8-inch) springform tin and line sides with baking parchment. Crush biscuits to make fine crumbs. Mix crumbs with melted butter and cinnamon. Press over base of pan and chill while you make the filling. In a measuring jug, combine lemon juice with enough orange juice or water to make 125 ml (4 fl oz). Sprinkle gelatin on top. Allow to soften for 5 minutes, then dissolve gelatin by microwaving on low power for 3–4 minutes. In a bowl, beat ricotta cheese, yogurt and half the sugar until smooth. Stir in lemon rind and dissolved gelatin. In another bowl, whisk egg whites until stiff, then whisk in remaining sugar. Fold whites into yogurt mixture and pour into crust. Smooth and chill for 3–4 hours or until set. To make the topping, arrange orange slices on top of cheesecake. Dissolve gelatin in orange juice (as you did before), allow to cool, then spoon juice over orange slices. Return cheesecake to fridge until set. To serve, transfer cheesecake to serving plate.

Serves 8

soured cream cheesecake with honeyed apricots

see variations page 76

Ricotta makes this baked cheesecake beautifully light, but if you want something slightly heavier and creamier, replace half the ricotta with full-fat cream cheese.

for the crust
200 g (7 oz) digestive biscuits
85 g (3 oz) unsalted butter, melted
for the cheesecake and topping
500 g (18 oz) ricotta cheese
175 g (6 oz) caster sugar
4 large eggs

1 tsp vanilla essence
225 g (8 oz) full-fat soured cream
for the honeyed apricots
175 g (6 oz) dried apricots, chopped
4 tbsp honey
1 tbsp lemon juice
55 g (2 oz) chopped walnuts

To make the crust, grease a 20-cm (8-inch) springform tin and line sides with baking parchment. Crush digestive biscuits until fine crumbs. Mix crumbs with melted butter, then press mixture over the base. Chill for 15 minutes. Preheat oven to 150°C (300°F/gas mark 2). To make the cheesecake, mix ricotta with half the sugar, then beat in eggs one at a time, followed by vanilla. Pour this mixture over the crust and place pan on a baking tray. Bake for 1 hour. Remove cheesecake from oven and allow to stand for 5 minutes. Stir remaining sugar into soured cream and pour over cheesecake. Return to oven for 5 minutes, then remove and allow to cool in pan. Chill until ready to serve. To make honeyed apricots, put apricots in a pan with honey, lemon juice and walnuts. Heat gently until honey melts. Cut cheesecake into slices and serve with the apricots spooned over. Apricots can be served warm or cold.

Serves 6–8

layered lime sponge with lemon icing

see variations page 77

Tangy, citrussyand with a deliciously moist texture, this sponge cake makes a lovely summer dessert when served with a selection of fresh fruits.

for the sponge
150 g (5½ oz) unsalted butter
150 g (5½ oz) light brown sugar
finely grated rind of 2 limes, plus a little extra
    to decorate
4 large eggs, separated
85 g (3 oz) plain flour

1 tsp baking powder
110 g (4 oz) ground almonds
for the icing
350 g full-fat cream cheese
3 tbsp lemon juice
150 g (5½ oz) icing sugar
fresh fruit, to serve

Grease and base line two 20-cm (8-inch) deep sandwich tins, Preheat oven to 180°C (350°F/ gas mark 4). To make the sponge cake, beat butter, sugar and lime rind together until light and creamy. Beat in egg yolks, one at a time. In a separate bowl, whisk egg whites until stiff. Sieve flour and baking powder into the creamed mixture and stir in along with ground almonds. Stir in a tablespoonful of egg whites, then fold in the rest using a large metal spoon. Divide mixture between cake tins and smooth tops level. Bake for about 30 minutes or until a cocktail stick pushed into cake comes out clean. Cool in pans for 10 minutes before turning out on to a wire rack to cool completely. To make the icing, beat cream cheese until smooth. Add lemon juice, sieve in icing sugar and beat until creamy. Spread one cake layer with some icing, place other layer on top and spread remaining icing over the top. Decorate with lime rind.

Serves 8

baked strawberry curd cake

see variations page 78

An English classic made from curd cheese. To keep the fruit from sinking, allow the mixture to stand for 10-15 minutes before baking, giving it a chance to thicken

for the base
55 g (2 oz) pecans
175 g (6 oz) digestive biscuits
85 g (3 oz) unsalted butter, melted
for the curd cake mixture
125 g (5½ oz) unsalted butter, softened
200 g (7 oz) light brown sugar
500 g (18 oz) curd, ricotta or quark cheese
4 large egg yolks

110 g (4 oz) ground almonds
55 g (2 oz) semolina
finely grated rind and juice of 1 large lemon
200 g (7 oz) fresh strawberries, hulled and
    coarsely chopped
1 tbsp plain flour
3 large egg whites
extra strawberries and icing sugar,
    to serve

°For the crust, preheat oven to 190°C (375°F/gas mark 5). Spread pecans on a baking tray and bake for 7–8 minutes until lightly toasted. Allow to cool and chop into small pieces. Grease a 23-cm (9-inch) springform tin and line sides with parchment. Crush digestive biscuits, transfer to a bowl, add pecans and melted butter and mix. Press mixture over base of tin and bake for 10 minutes. To make curd mixture, in a large bowl, beat butter until creamy, add sugar and cheese and beat until smooth. Stir in egg yolks, one at a time and add almonds, semolina, lemon rind and juice. Toss chopped strawberries in flour and fold in. Let mixture stand for 10–15 minutes. In a separate bowl, whisk egg whites until they stand in stiff peaks. Stir 1 tablespoon into cake mixture before folding in the rest. Pour into prepared tin and bake for about 1 hour or until firm. Allow to cool completely, then remove from tin. Chill until ready to serve. Just before serving, top with sliced strawberries and dust with icing sugar.
Serves 10

banoffee cheesecake

see variations page 79

Leaving the cheesecake to cool slowly in the oven will help prevent the top from cracking, but if it does, just cover the cracks with cream when you decorate it.

for the crust
175 g (6 oz) digestive biscuits
25 g (1 oz) walnuts, finely chopped
55 g (2 oz) unsalted butter, melted
for the cheesecake topping
3 ripe bananas
juice of ½ lemon
5 tbsp dulce de leche
3 large eggs

500 g (18 oz) ricotta cheese
85 g (3 oz) light brown sugar
to decorate
110 g (4 oz) granulated sugar
2 tbsp water
250 ml (8 fl oz) whipping cream
1 tsp coffee essence
1 small banana, sliced
juice of ½ lemon

To make the crust, mix biscuit crumbs with walnuts and melted butter. Press mixture over base of a lightly greased 20-cm (8-inch) springform tin and chill. Preheat the oven to 150°C (300°F/gas mark 2). Peel bananas and roughly chop. Place in a food processor with lemon juice, dulce de leche, eggs, ricotta and sugar. Blend until smooth. Pour mixture into crust and bake for 50–60 minutes or until firm. Turn off oven and leave cheesecake inside to cool. For decorations, line a baking tray with baking parchment. Dissolve sugar with water in a pan over a gentle heat. Bring to the boil and allow to syrup turn golden amber. Drizzle small caramel shapes onto parchment with a spoon and harden. Transfer cheesecake to serving plate when cooled. Whip cream with coffee essence, spread a thin layer over the top of cheesecake. Pipe or spoon remaining cream around the top edge and chill. Just before serving, decorate with caramel shapes and banana slices tossed in lemon juice.

Serves 6-8

sticky toffee sponges with fudge sauce

see variations page 80

A classic English dessert that's warm and comforting when the weather is cold. The soft crumbly sponge makes the perfect foil for the creamy fudge sauce.

for the fudge sauce
85 g (3 oz) unsalted butter
110 g (4 oz) dark brown sugar
200 ml (7 fl oz) crème fraîche
6 tbsp water
for the sponges
½ tsp bicarbonate of soda
110 g (4 oz) raisins

1 tbsp treacle
125 ml (4 fl oz) boiling water
65 g (2½ oz) unsalted butter, softened
65 g (2½ oz) dark brown sugar
1 large egg, beaten
125 g (4½ oz) self-raising flour
1 tsp ground ginger
85 g (3 oz) chopped walnuts

Lightly grease six mini pudding basins or ramekins. To make the sauce, place butter, sugar and crème fraîche in a pan and add water. Heat gently until butter and sugar melt, then bring to the boil and simmer for 2 minutes. Remove from heat and pour 1 tablespoon into each basin. Preheat oven to 180°C (350°F/gas mark 4). Put bicarbonate of soda, raisins and treacle in a bowl. Pour over boiling water. In another bowl, beat butter and sugar together until creamy, then beat in egg. Stir in raisin mixture, flour, ginger and two-thirds of the walnuts. Spoon mixture into basins, place on a baking tray and bake for 35 minutes. Allow to stand while you reheat sauce; they'll be easier to turn out after standing. Turn puddings out onto serving plates and scatter remaining walnuts on top. Pour reheated sauce over them and serve at once.

Serves 6

lemon & polenta sponge with blueberry sauce

see variations page 81

The secret ingredient in this light, fruity sponge is the whole lemons, which are cooked whole, then puréed. It's best to use lemons with thin skins, as too much pith between the zest and fruit will make the cake taste bitter.

for the sponge
2 lemons
3 large eggs
200 g (7 oz) light brown sugar
110 g (4 oz) fine polenta
140 g (5 oz) semolina

1 tsp baking powder
icing sugar, to dust
for the blueberry sauce
350 g (12 oz) blueberries, plus extra to serve
2 tbsp light brown sugar

To make the sponge, put lemons in a pan, cover with water and bring to the boil. Cover pan and simmer for about 45 minutes or until lemons are soft. Drain and cool, then cut lemons in half and remove seeds. Place lemons in a food processor and purée. Grease a 20-cm (8-inch) springform tin and line with parchment. Preheat oven to 180° (350°F/gas mark 4). Whisk eggs and sugar in a bowl until thick, creamy and pale. Fold in polenta, semolina, baking powder and lemon purée. Pour mixture into tin and bake for 45–50 minutes or until a cocktail stick inserted in the centre comes out clean. Allow to cool for at least 30 minutes before removing from tin. To make blueberry sauce, gently heat about three-quarters of the berries in a pan with sugar, crushing with a fork or spoon until their juices run. Purée in a food processor, return to pan and stir in reserved berries. Serve the sponge, warm or cold, dusted with icing sugar and sliced. Accompany with warmed sauce and blueberries.
Serves 8

butterscotch apple sponge

see variations page 82

Another English specialty that combines a fruit-topped sponge with a rich, toffee-litreike sauce. You'll need to use a heatproof bowl and cook the sponge in a steamer. Serve with extra stewed apples if you like.

for the butterscotch sauce
85 g (3 oz) unsalted butter
85 g (3 oz) light brown sugar
85 ml (3 fl oz) golden syrup
1 tbsp lemon juice
125 ml (4 fl oz) double cream

for the sponge
1 apple, such as Granny Smith, peeled, cored
    and chopped
175 g (6 oz) unsalted butter, softened
175 g (6 oz) light brown sugar
3 large eggs
175 g (6 oz) plain flour
1 tsp baking powder
1 tsp ground ginger

Grease a 2.5-litre (4-pint) pudding basin or other heatproof bowl such as Pyrex. To make the sauce, heat butter, sugar and golden syrup together in a pan, simmering gently until melted. Remove from heat and stir in lemon juice followed by cream. Spoon 2 tablespoons of sauce into greased bowl and set the rest aside. Add chopped apples. To make the sponge. In a mixing bowl, beat butter and sugar until creamy, then beat in eggs, one at a time, adding a tablespoon of flour with each one. Sieve in remaining flour, baking powder and ginger. Fold everything together until evenly combined. Spoon mixture into dish and smooth the top level. Cover tightly with waxed paper and foil and steam for 1½ hours. Check water level in steamer regularly and add boiling water as necessary. Turn out sponge on a serving plate, cut into slices and serve with remaining warmed butterscotch sauce poured over.

Serves 6

pear & raspberry clafoutis

see variations page 83

Not strictly a sponge or a hot soufflé, this classic French batter pudding falls somewhere between. The fluffy batter mixture puffs up and becomes lighter in the oven and contrasts well with the sweet pears and sharper-flavoured raspberries.

25 g (1 oz) unsalted butter, melted, plus extra
    for greasing
3 ripe but firm pears, peeled, cored and sliced
110 g (4 oz) fresh raspberries
85 g (3 oz) plain flour

85 g (3 oz) caster sugar
4 large eggs
350 ml (12 fl oz) milk
1 tsp vanilla essence

Grease a 1-litre (2-pint) shallow ovenproof dish with melted butter and arrange pear slices and raspberries in it. Preheat oven to 190°C (375°F/gas mark 5). Mix flour and sugar together in a bowl. In a separate bowl, beat eggs, milk and vanilla. Gradually whisk egg mixture into flour and sugar until evenly mixed and you have a light, creamy batter. Fold in 2 tablespoons melted butter. Pour batter carefully into baking dish over fruit and bake for 40–45 minutes or until risen and golden brown. Serve warm on its own or with cream.

Serves 6

hot orange soufflé

see variations page 84

Not many desserts need to be served immediately after they come out of the oven, but soufflés most certainly do. If you delay, the soft, fluffy cloud will collapse.

25 g (1 oz) unsalted butter, plus extra
    for greasing
25 g (1 oz) plain flour
350 ml (12 fl oz) milk
finely grated rind and juice of 1 large orange
110 g (4 oz) caster sugar
4 large egg yolks
5 large egg whites

icing sugar, to dust
for the orange sauce
110 g (4 oz) caster sugar
1 tbsp cornflour
finely grated rind and juice of 1 medium orange
250 ml (8 fl oz) water
25 g (1 oz) unsalted butter

Melt butter in a medium-litrearge saucepan. When butter has melted, stir in flour off the heat, then cook gently for 1 minute. Gradually stir in milk off the heat, then whisk continuously over medium heat until mixture is thickened. Stir in orange rind and juice. Stir in three-quarters of the sugar and scatter remaining sugar over the top. Grease 1.5-litre (2½-pint) soufflé dish with melted butter. Preheat oven to 180°C (350°F/gas mark 4). Beat egg yolks into cooled soufflé mixture one at a time. Whisk whites until stiff. Stir 1 tablespoon whites into soufflé mixture before folding in the rest. Pour mixture into soufflé dish. With a knife, cut through mixture about 2.5 cm (1 inch) from edge to help soufflé rise evenly. Bake for 45–50 minutes or until firm on top but springy in the centre. Meanwhile, for the sauce: mix sugar, cornflour, orange rind and water until smooth. Heat gently, stirring constantly, until sauce is thick and smooth. Simmer for 30 seconds, then remove from heat and stir in butter and orange juice. When soufflé is cooked, dust top with icing sugar and serve immediately with hot orange sauce.
Serves 4

individual raspberry soufflés

see variations page 85

If you don't have ramekins, you could use ovenproof tea or coffee cups or other containers with straight sides. The shape of the cups is important, because if the sides slope outward the soufflés won't rise properly.

275 g (10 oz) fresh raspberries
juice of 1 lemon
125 g (4½ oz) caster sugar
1½ tbsp cornflour, mixed with 2 tbsp water
   until smooth

a little melted butter for greasing
3 large egg yolks
4 large egg whites
icing sugar, to dust

Put raspberries in a pan, add lemon juice and half the sugar and simmer for 2 minutes or until they are soft and falling apart. Remove from heat and push through a wire sieve to remove seeds. Return purée to saucepan and mix in cornflour mixture. Cook over medium heat, stirring constantly, until purée is thick and smooth. Transfer to a bowl and set aside to cool completely. Preheat oven to 190°C (375°F/gas mark 5). Grease six 200-ml (7-fl oz) ramekins with melted butter. Stir egg yolks one at a time into raspberry purée. In another bowl, whisk egg whites until stiff, add remaining sugar and whisk until glossy. Stir a tablespoonful of whites into raspberry mixture, before carefully folding in the rest. Spoon into ramekins, smooth tops level and run a small knife around the top edge of each, between the ramekin and the mixture, to help soufflés rise evenly. Set ramekins on a baking tray and bake for 8-10 minutes or until set and crusty on top but still soft in the middle. Remove from oven, dust tops with icing sugar and serve at once.

Serves 6

citrus cheesecake with ginger crumb crust

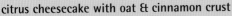

see base recipe page 59

citrus cheesecake with oat & cinnamon crust
Prepare basic recipe, using oat-based biscuits and ground cinnamon for the base rather than gingersnaps.

rich citrus cream cheesecake with ginger crumb crust
Prepare basic recipe, replacing ricotta cheese with cream cheese and half the yogurt with double or whipping cream for a richer result. Whip cream until it just holds its shape and fold in before adding whisked egg whites.

baked cheesecake with mixed citrus fruits
Prepare basic recipe, topping the cheesecake with mixed citrus fruits such as grapefruit, kumquat and tangerine as well as or instead of orange slices.

citrus cheesecake with seeded crust
Prepare basic recipe, replacing gingersnaps with digestive biscuits for the base, reducing quantity by 2 tablespoons and stirring in 2 tablespoons of seeds such as sesame, pumpkin, poppy or sunflower with the butter, omitting the cinnamon.

red fruit cheesecake with ginger crumb crust
Prepare basic recipe, topping cheesecake with raspberries or sliced strawberries instead of orange and dissolving gelatin in cranberry juice instead of orange.

variations

soured cream cheesecake with honeyed apricots

see base recipe page 60

soured cream cheesecake with sponge base
Prepare basic recipe, replacing crumb base with sponge. Beat together
110 grams (4 ounces) each of unsalted butter and caster sugar until creamy.
Beat in 2 large eggs and stir in 110 g (4 ounces) self-raising flour. Bake for
15–20 minutes at 190°C (375°F/gas mark 5).

soured cream cheesecake with honeyed mixed fruits & nuts
Prepare basic recipe for the honeyed apricots, using a mix of dried fruits
such as raisins, cranberries or mango in place of apricots; maple syrup
instead of honey; and pecans instead of walnuts.

soured cream lemon cheesecake
Prepare basic recipe, replacing vanilla with the finely grated rind of 1 lemon.

soured cream cheesecake with honeyed fresh fruits
Prepare basic recipe for the honeyed apricots, using fresh fruit such as
chopped apples, pears or peaches instead of dried apricots, simmering with
the honey until softened.

soured cream cheesecake with peanut crust & honeyed apricots
Prepare basic recipe, replacing 25 grams (1 ounce) digestive biscuits with
finely chopped unsalted peanuts.

layered lime sponge with lemon icing

see base recipe page 62

layered lemon sponge with lemon icing
Prepare basic recipe, replacing lime rind in sponge with rind of 1 large lemon.

layered lime & cashew sponge with lemon icing
Prepare basic recipe, replacing ground almonds in sponge with ground cashews.

layered lime sponge with maple icing
Prepare basic recipe, replacing cream cheese icing with a maple-flavoured one. Heat 1 tablespoon maple syrup with 55 grams (2 ounces) unsalted butter and 1 tablespoon milk until butter melts. Sieve 225 grams (8 ounces) icing sugar and mix with melted mixture until smooth. Cool, then beat with a wooden spoon or whisk until thick enough to spread.

layered lime sponge with oranges & lemon icing
Prepare basic recipe, adding segments of 2 oranges between cake layers.

layered lime sponge with citrus buttercream
Prepare basic recipe, replacing icing with lime or lemon buttercream. Beat 200 grams (7 ounces) unsalted butter with finely grated rind of 2 limes or 1 large lemon and 200 grams (7 ounces) sieved icing sugar until smooth. Stir in lime or lemon juice until soft and spreadable.

variations

baked strawberry curd cake

see base recipe page 64

baked raspberry curd cake
Prepare basic recipe, replacing strawberries with raspberries.

baked strawberry curd cake with lemon cream
Prepare basic recipe, adding a topping of whipped cream rather than dusting with icing sugar. Whip 200 ml (7 fl oz) whipping cream until it just holds its shape. Lightly fold in 3 tablespoons lemon curd until it is just streaked with lemon curd. Spoon lemon cream over the cake, spreading in an even layer and top with extra whole strawberries just before serving.

baked strawberry curd cake with a nutty crust
Prepare basic recipe, replacing pecans in crust with walnuts or hazelnuts.

baked strawberry & orange curd cake
Prepare basic recipe, replacing lemon rind and juice in curd mixture with rind and juice of 1 small orange.

baked peach curd cake
Prepare basic recipe, replacing chopped strawberries in curd mixture with chopped flesh of 2 peeled and stoned ripe peaches.

banoffee cheesecake

see base recipe page 65

banoffee cheesecake with pecan crust
Prepare basic recipe, replacing walnuts in crust with finely chopped pecans
(almonds also work well).

banoffee cheesecake with toffee sauce
Prepare basic recipe and serve with toffee sauce. To make gently heat 85 grams
(3 ounces) unsalted butter with 175 grams (6 ounces) brown sugar and 125 ml
(4 fl oz) golden syrup until melted. Simmer for 4–5 minutes, stir in 175 ml
(6 fl oz) double cream and ½ teaspoon vanilla until smooth. Cool before serving
with cheesecake.

banoffee cheesecake with dulce de leche cream
Prepare basic recipe, whisking 2 tablespoons dulce de leche into the cream for
decoration instead of the coffee essence.

banoffee cheesecake with chocolate crumb crust
Prepare basic recipe, replacing digestive biscuits with chocolate chip biscuits,
ground to crumbs.

rich banoffee & orange cheesecake
Prepare basic recipe, replacing half the ricotta with cream cheese for a richer
filling and the lemon juice in the filling with 2 tablespoons orange juice.

variations

sticky toffee sponges with fudge sauce

see base recipe page 66

sticky toffee sponges with lemon cream sauce
Prepare basic recipe, replacing fudge sauce with a sharper-flavoured lemon cream sauce. To make it, heat 350 ml (12 fl oz) single cream in a pan with the finely grated rind of 2 lemons and 55 grams (2 ounces) icing sugar until sugar dissolves and mixture comes to the boil. Bubble gently for 5 minutes until the sauce thickens a little. Serve warm.

sticky toffee sponges with prunes
Prepare basic recipe, replacing raisins with chopped stoned prunes.

sticky toffee sponges with sweet spice
Prepare basic recipe, flavouring pudding with 1 teaspoon ground cardamom or ground cinnamon instead of ginger.

sticky toffee sponges with pecans
Prepare basic recipe, using chopped pecans instead of walnuts.

sticky toffee sponges with orange
Prepare basic recipe, replacing ground ginger with finely grated rind of 1 orange.

variations

lemon & polenta sponge with blueberry sauce

see base recipe page 68

lemon & polenta sponge with crème fraîche
Prepare basic recipe, omitting blueberry sauce. Let sponge cool, then spread with crème fraîche and scatter top with toasted flaked almonds and blueberries.

orange & polenta sponge
Prepare basic recipe, replacing lemons with 1 medium orange or 3 clementines. Simmer orange for 1 hour (clementines for 45 minutes).

lemon & polenta sponge with strawberry sauce
Prepare basic recipe, replacing blueberries with strawberries.

lemon & semolina sponge
If you don't like the texture of polenta, omit polenta and use 250 grams (9 ounces) semolina.

lemon & polenta sponge with caramelised oranges
Prepare basic recipe, serving sponge with caramelised oranges instead of blueberry sauce. Remove peel and pith from 6 oranges. Slice fruit into thin rounds, removing any seeds. Gently heat 175 grams (6 ounces) caster sugar with 125 ml (4 fl oz) orange juice, orange liqueur or water to dissolve sugar. Bring to the boil and cook to a golden caramel. Add orange slices and any juices they made and simmer for 2 minutes. Allow to cool.

variations

butterscotch apple sponge

see base recipe page 70

butterscotch pear sponge
Prepare basic recipe, replacing apple with 1 pear.

apple sponge with apple sauce
Prepare basic recipe, replacing butterscotch sauce with apple sauce. Over low heat, cook 500 grams (1 pound) peeled and sliced apples with 2 tablespoons water and 1 tablespoon lemon juice. When soft, mash and add sugar and butter to taste.

butterscotch apple & honey sponge
Prepare basic recipe. Replace 2 tablespoons sugar in the sponge with honey.

spicy butterscotch apple sponge
Prepare basic recipe, replacing ginger in sponge with ground cinnamon or mixed spice.

butterscotch apple sponge with maple cream sauce
Prepare basic recipe, replacing butterscotch sauce with creamy maple sauce. Melt 85 grams (3 ounces) unsalted butter, add 150 grams (5 ounces) light brown sugar and 2 tablespoons maple syrup. When sugar dissolves, add 7 tablespoons double cream. Bring to the boil, remove from heat and spoon 2 tablespoons into dish. Serve the rest warm with sponge.

variations

pear & raspberry clafoutis

see base recipe page 71

peach & blueberry clafoutis
Prepare basic recipe, replacing pears with 3 large ripe firm peaches or 350 grams (12 ounces) halved stoned plums and raspberries with blueberries.

creamy pear & raspberry clafoutis
For a richer dessert, prepare basic recipe replacing 125 ml (4 fl oz) milk with light or whipping cream.

pear & raspberry clafoutis with sweet spices
Prepare basic recipe, replacing vanilla with 1 teaspoon ground cinnamon, mixed spice or ginger.

pear & raspberry chocolate clafoutis
Prepare basic recipe, replacing 1 tablespoon flour with 1 tablespoon cocoa powder, dissolved in 1 tablespoon hot water, for a chocolate batter. Add the cocoa with the melted butter and fold in evenly.

pear & raspberry soufflé clafoutis
For a lighter, more soufflé-litreike batter, prepare basic recipe, separating the eggs. Beat just the yolks with milk and vanilla. Whisk whites until snowy peaks and fold in after the melted butter.

variations

hot orange soufflé

see base recipe page 72

hot orange & chocolate soufflé
Prepare basic recipe, drizzling 55 grams (2 ounces) melted plain chocolate
over soufflé when it comes out of oven. Omit orange sauce.

hot lemon soufflé
Prepare basic recipe, replacing orange with 2 lemons.

hot orange soufflés in orange shells
Prepare basic recipe. Slice tops off 6 large oranges and scoop out flesh.
Strain, use 4 tablespoons of the juice for the recipe, plus finely grated rind
from the tops of the oranges. Cut a thin slice off base of each orange shell
and stand in a greased ovenproof dish. Spoon soufflé mixture into shells.
Bake at 200°C (400°F/gas mark 6) for 20–25 minutes until risen and golden.

hot herby orange soufflé
Prepare basic recipe, stirring in 1 tablespoon finely chopped fresh basil or
rosemary with orange rind and juice.

hot chocolate soufflé
For a hot chocolate soufflé, prepare basic recipe, increasing milk to 600 ml
(1-pint) and omitting orange rind and juice. Stir 85 grams (3 ounces) grated
plain chocolate into hot milk before adding sugar.

individual raspberry soufflés

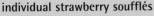

see base recipe page 74

individual strawberry soufflés
Prepare basic recipe, using strawberries instead of raspberries. There is no need to strain the purée.

individual raspberry & mint soufflés
Prepare basic recipe, stirring 1 tablespoon finely chopped fresh mint into the strained raspberry purée before adding egg yolks.

individual raspberry soufflés with mango sauce
Prepare basic recipe, serving hot soufflés with mango sauce. Peel 1 ripe mango and put flesh in a liquidiser or food processor. Add 125 ml (4 fl oz) freshly squeezed orange juice and blend until smooth. Add more orange juice to make a smooth sauce if the mango is large. Warm sauce and when soufflés come out of oven, place on serving plates, push a hole in the centre of each with a spoon and pour in warm sauce.

individual blackberry soufflés
Prepare basic recipe, replacing raspberries with blackberries.

individual fruits-of-the-forest soufflés
Prepare basic recipe, using a mixture of berries and currants of your choice. If not too many seedy fruits such as raspberries are included, there's no need to strain.

pies, crumbles & tarts

Well-loved family favourites that will never cease to impress. Whether your taste is for a simple fruit crumble, a wickedly rich chocolate and peanut butter pie or light and crisp filo tarts, you'll find lots of irresistible ideas in this chapter.

strawberry cream pie

see variations page 103

A gorgeous taste of summer, this pie would be perfect for a party in the garden on a sunny day. Do not add the sliced strawberries for decoration until just before serving or juices will run from the fruit and spoil the appearance of the crème fraîche.

for the crust
300 g (11 oz) amaretti biscuits
85 g (3 oz) plain chocolate, chopped
110 g (4 oz) unsalted butter, melted
for the filling
225 g (8 oz) fresh strawberries, hulled and
    roughly chopped

4 large eggs
110 g (4 oz) caster sugar
125 ml (4 fl oz) double cream
for the topping
125 g (4 fl oz) crème fraîche
extra strawberries, sliced

Preheat oven to 180°C (350°F/gas mark 4). To make the crust, crush amaretti in a food processor to make coarse crumbs. Add chocolate and process again until mixture is quite fine. Transfer to a bowl and stir in melted butter. Press crumb mixture over base and sides of a 23-cm (9-inch) loose-bottomed flan tin or pie dish measuring about 4 cm (1½ inches) deep. Place tin on a baking tray and bake for 10 minutes. Remove from oven and push crust down with the back of a spoon if it has risen up. To make the filling, put strawberries, eggs and sugar in a food processor or liquidiser. Blend until smooth. In a bowl, whip cream to soft peaks, then fold in strawberry purée until evenly mixed. Pour filling into crust and bake for 25 minutes or until set. Remove from oven and cool completely before removing from pan. Spread crème fraîche over pie. Chill until ready to serve. Decorate with sliced strawberries just before serving.

Serves 8

deep-dish nectarine & blueberry pie

see variations page 104

A great dessert when you've got the family to feed, it's filling and deliciously fruity.

for the pastry
225 g (8 oz) plain flour
150 g (5 oz) unsalted butter, cut in small pieces
2 tbsp caster sugar, plus extra to dust
1 egg yolk
3 tbsp cold water
beaten egg, to glaze

for the filling
about 6 ripe nectarines (depending on size),
    peeled, stoned and sliced
225 g (8 oz) fresh blueberries
1 tbsp caster sugar

To make the pastry, sieve flour into a mixing bowl. Rub in butter until mixture resembles breadcrumbs. Stir in sugar. Beat egg yolk with water and add to bowl, mixing in to make a dough. Knead lightly until smooth, wrap in clingfilm and chill for 30 minutes. Arrange sliced nectarines and blueberries in a small pie dish. Roll out pastry, cut a strip about 2.5 cm (1 inch) wide to fit around top edge of pie dish, dampen and press in place. Lift remaining pastry over fruit, trimming edges with a sharp knife. Press pastry edges together to seal and mark a decorative border with the back of a knife. Gather up and reroll pastry trimmings and cut out leaves with a small sharp knife. Dampen and arrange these over pie. Cut a hole in pastry top to allow steam to escape. When ready to bake, preheat oven to 180°C (350°F/ gas mark 4). Brush pastry with beaten egg to glaze and dust with sugar. Set pie on baking tray and bake for 35 minutes or until golden brown. Serve warm or cold with whipped cream or ice cream.

Serves 6

chocolate-glazed peanut butter & cinnamon pie

see variations page 105

Chocolate and peanut butter are a marriage made in heaven in this wickedly rich dessert. If you don't have a pie plate, use an 20-cm (8-inch) flan tin instead.

for the crust
200 g (7 oz) chocolate digestive biscuits
85 g (3 oz) unsalted butter, melted
for the pie
250 ml (9 fl oz) single cream cheese
150 oz (5½ oz) crunchy peanut butter
55 g (2 oz) light brown sugar

½ tsp ground cinnamon
250 ml (8 fl oz) double cream
25 g (1 oz) unsalted butter
55 g (2 oz) plain chocolate, chopped
extra whipped cream, chocolate sticks or
    cigarillos and grated chocolate, to decorate

To make the crust, crush digestive biscuits to fine crumbs and mix with melted butter. Press mixture over base and up sides of a 23-cm (9-inch) pie plate. Chill while you prepare filling. To make the filling, whisk together cream cheese, peanut butter, brown sugar and cinnamon. In another bowl, whip cream until it starts to thicken. Stir about ²/₃ of the whipped cream into peanut butter mixture. Spoon into crumb crust and smooth out until level.

Put butter, chocolate and remaining whipped cream in a saucepan and heat gently until butter and chocolate melt. Stir until smooth, cool, then pour over the filling. Chill for at least 1 hour to firm. When ready to serve, decorate with extra whipped cream, chocolate curls and chocolate sticks or cigarillos and a sprinkling of grated chocolate.

Serves 8

apricot–pistachio tarte tatin

see variations page 106

A variation on the famous French tart named after the sisters who, so the story goes, cooked their favourite apple tart upside down by mistake. When inverting the cooked tart onto a serving plate, be sure the plate is large enough to prevent any hot caramel splashing over your hands.

110 g (4 oz) caster sugar
55 g (2 oz) unsalted butter, chopped small
500 g (18 oz) fresh apricots, halved and stoned

350 g (12 oz) puff pastry, defrosted if frozen
55 g (2 oz) pistachios
crème fraîche, to serve

Heat sugar and butter in a 23-cm (9-inch) tarte tatin tin or ovenproof frying pan until melted, then cook to a rich golden brown caramel. Remove pan from heat and arrange apricot halves, rounded-side down, in pan almost to edge. Place first one at a slight angle and the rest butting up against each other and overlapping slightly to allow for shrinkage during baking. Work from outside into centre, placing apricots in concentric circles until tin is full.

Preheat the oven to 190°C (375°F/gas mark 5). Roll out pastry on a lightly floured surface to a circle the same size as the tin. Lift it over apricots, tucking pastry edges down the sides between apricots and tin. Prick pastry all over with a fork and place tin on a baking tray. Bake for 25–30 minutes or until pastry is puffed and golden brown. Remove tin from oven and let stand for 2–3 minutes before inverting tart onto a warm serving plate. Tuck back into place any apricots that stick to the tin and scatter pistachios over top. Serve warm with crème fraîche.

Serves 6

plum frangipane tarts

see variations page 107

Frangipane is a sweet almond sponge mixture that is popular in France, where it is added to several classic desserts such as these fruit flans. If you don't have individual flan tins, make one large one using a 20- or 23-cm (8- or 9-inch) tin.

for the pastry
55 g (2 oz) caster sugar
65 g (2½ oz) unsalted butter, cut up
1 large egg yolk
2 tbsp cold water
175 g (6 oz) plain flour
for the filling
8 tbsp plum jam

160 g (5½ oz) ground almonds
100 g (3½ oz) caster sugar
finely grated rind of 1 lemon
3 large eggs, beaten
5 tbsp sunflower oil
4 tbsp freshly squeezed orange juice
8 plums, stoned and sliced
2 tbsp chopped toasted hazelnuts

To make the pastry, put sugar, butter and egg yolk in a food processor, and blend until smooth. Add water and blend again. Add flour and blend until ingredients are just combined. Knead dough lightly on a lightly floured work surface until smooth. Shape into a ball, wrap in clingfilm and chill for 1 hour. Bring back to room temperature before rolling out. Preheat oven to 180°C (350°F/gas mark 4). Divide pastry into 4 pieces. Roll out each piece on a lightly floured surface and line four individual flan tins. Place on a greased baking tray. Spread 1 tablespoon plum jam over the base of each pastry crust. To make the filling, whisk together ground almonds, sugar, lemon rind, eggs, oil and orange juice until smooth. Spoon into crusts. Top with plum slices, pressing them down gently and bake for 25–30 minutes or until almond mixture is golden and set. Remove tarts from oven. Warm remaining jam and brush over top of each tart. Sprinkle with toasted hazelnuts and serve warm.

Serves 4

cherry & custard filo tarts

see variations page 108

Once unwrapped, filo pastry dries out very quickly and becomes too hard and brittle to use, so work as quickly as you can.

32 squares filo pastry, each about 10-cm
   (4 inches)
110 g (4 oz) unsalted butter, melted
for the custard
2 large eggs
1 large egg yolk
55 g (2 oz) caster sugar

1 tbsp cornflour
200 ml (7 fl oz) crème fraîche
½ tsp vanilla essence
for the cherries
350 g (12 oz) ripe cherries, stoned
4 tbsp orange juice
1 tbsp caster sugar or to taste

Brush a filo square with melted butter, press gently into a cup in a muffin tin. Repeat, layering 3 more squares on top and angling the points of the squares in a star pattern. Repeat with remaining filo squares to make 8 crusts. Bake for 15–20 minutes or until pastry is golden brown. Remove from oven and cool for 10–15 minutes before lifting crusts from tin. Allow to cool completely. To make the custard, put eggs, egg yolk and 3 tablespoons sugar in a bowl. Beat until pale and creamy. Stir in cornflour. Bring crème fraîche to the boil, then pour onto egg mixture, whisking constantly. Return mixture to pan and slowly bring to the boil over low heat, stirring constantly. Cook gently for 2–3 minutes then remove from heat. Stir in vanilla and sprinkle remaining sugar over top of custard to prevent a skin forming. When cold, chill until needed. Put cherries in a small pan with orange juice and sugar, cover and simmer gently for 10 minutes or until softened; cool. When ready to serve, stir custard well, fill filo crusts and set on serving plates. Drain cherries and spoon them on top of custard.

Serves 8

french apple tart

see variations page 109

To make the pastry by hand, sieve the flour into a bowl and make a well in the centre. Place the butter and egg yolk in the well and mix to a coarse paste. Draw the flour over egg mixture and chop through with a palette knife. Sprinkle with water and bring the dough together with your hands, kneading until smooth.

for the pastry
100 g (3½ oz) unsalted butter at room
    temperature, cut into small pieces
1 medium egg yolk
2½ tbsp cold water
200 g (7 oz) plain flour
for the filling
4 apples, such as Golden Delicious or Braeburn

3 tbsp caster sugar
1 tsp ground cinnamon
55 g (2 oz) unsalted butter, cut into small
    pieces
for the glaze
4 tbsp apricot jam
1 tbsp lemon juice

To make the pastry, blend butter and egg yolk in food processor until smooth and creamy. Add water and blend again. Pour in flour and pulse briefly until dough just comes together in a ball. Transfer to a lightly floured work surface and knead gently until smooth. Wrap in clingfilm and chill for 45 minutes. Allow pastry to return to room temperature before rolling out and lining a 23-cm (9-inch) loose-bottomed flan tin. To make the filling, peel, core and thinly slice apples. Spread half the apples randomly over pastry, then top with remaining apple slices arranged in neat concentric circles, overlapping to fill shell completely. Sprinkle with sugar and cinnamon and dot with butter. Preheat oven to 190°C (375°F/gas mark 5). Bake tart on a baking tray for about 50–60 minutes or until apples are browned and pastry is golden. Remove from oven and stand for 10 minutes before lifting tart from tin. Heat apricot jam and lemon juice until bubbling. Strain, then brush over apple slices to glaze.
Serves 6

kiwi, orange & white chocolate cream mille-feuille

see variations page 110

When you roll out the pastry, be careful not to stretch it or it will shrink back during baking and the mille-feuille layers will be uneven. Do not assemble these more than two hours before serving or the pastry will become soft.

350 g (12 oz) puff pastry
icing sugar, to dust
for the filling
125 ml (4 fl oz) double cream

150 g (5 oz) white chocolate, chopped
2 kiwi fruit, peeled and sliced
4 oranges, peeled and segmented

Line a baking tray with baking parchment. On a board dusted with icing sugar, roll out pastry about 6 mm (¼ inch thick). Using a sharp knife, cut out 12 rectangles, each about 8x5 cm (3½x2 inches). Lift them onto baking tray, dust with icing sugar and chill for 30 minutes. Preheat oven to 200°C (400°F/gas mark 6).

Bake pastry rectangles for 5 minutes, remove from oven and dust with more icing sugar. Return to oven and bake for 5 minutes more or until pastry is risen and golden brown. Transfer to a wire rack and allow to cool. To make the filling, bring cream to the boil, remove from heat and stir in white chocolate until just melted. Allow to cool, stirring occasionally. When thick enough to spread, whisk for 1 minute until light and creamy. Using a sharp knife, split each pastry rectangle in half horizontally and spread or pipe chocolate cream over the bases. Top with fruit and pastry lids. Dust with more icing sugar and chill until ready to serve.
Serves 6

blackberry & apple oatmeal crumble

see variations page 111

This crumble, with its crunchy oat topping and spicy fruit filling, makes a great family dessert.

700 g (1½ lbs) cooking apples, peeled, cored
   and chopped
finely grated rind and juice of 1 orange
1 tsp mixed spice
25 g (1 oz) caster sugar
225 g (8 oz) fresh blackberries

for the topping
110 g (4 oz) unsalted butter, cut up
   into small pieces
110 g (4 oz) plain flour
110 g (4 oz) chopped walnuts
55 g (2 oz) rolled oats
85 g (3 oz) light brown sugar

Place chopped apples in a saucepan. Add orange rind and juice, mixed spice and sugar and simmer over low heat for 10 minutes or until apples have softened. Gently stir in blackberries taking care not to crush them. Spoon fruit into a 1½-litre (2-pint) ovenproof dish and allow to cool completely.

To make the topping, rub butter into flour until consistency is like fine breadcrumbs. Stir in walnuts, oats and sugar. Spoon mixture over fruit to cover it evenly. Preheat oven to 180°C (350°F/gas mark 4) and bake for 35 minutes or until topping is golden. Serve hot with custard (pages 24–25).

Serves 8

strawberry cream pie

see base recipe page 87

strawberry cream pie with biscuit crust
Prepare basic recipe, replacing amaretti in crust with a digestive biscuits or chocolate digestive biscuits.

blueberry cream pie
Prepare basic recipe, using whole fresh blueberries instead of strawberries.

strawberry cream pie with strawberry sauce
Prepare basic recipe, serving with strawberry sauce rather than crème fraîche. Hull 350 grams (12 ounces) fresh strawberries. Purée 250 grams (8 ounces) in a food processor or liquidiser with 4 tablespoons orange juice and 2 tablespoons icing sugar. Stir in remaining strawberries, chopped in small pieces.

strawberry & lime cream pie
Prepare basic recipe, adding finely grated rind of 2 limes to filling. (You could use rind from 1 lemon instead, if you want.)

strawberry cream pie with chocolate cream
Prepare basic recipe, replacing crème fraîche topping with chocolate cream. Dissolve 1 tablespoon unsweetened cocoa in 1 tablespoon hot water, cool, then add to whipped cream.

variations

deep-dish nectarine & blueberry pie

see base recipe page 88

deep-dish pear & blackberry pie
Prepare basic recipe, replacing nectarines with pears and blueberries with
blackberries (or raspberries).

deep-dish nectarine & blueberry pie with
cinnamon whole-wheat crust
Prepare basic recipe, making the pastry with half wholemeal flour and half
self-raising white flour and adding 1 teaspoon ground cinnamon.

deep-dish spiced nectarine & blueberry pie
Prepare basic recipe, adding 1 teaspoon ground ginger and ½ teaspoon
ground cinnamon to fruit.

creamy deep-dish nectarine & blueberry pie
Prepare basic recipe, adding 4 tablespoons double cream to fruit.

deep-dish pineapple & blueberry pie
Prepare basic recipe, using 500 grams (1 pound) each of nectarines and
pineapple (or mango) plus the blueberries for filling.

chocolate-glazed peanut butter & cinnamon pie

see base recipe page 90

peanut butter & cinnamon pie with chocolate sauce & ice cream
Prepare basic recipe, omitting chocolate topping (or using it if you really
want the extra decadence). Serve with hot or cold chocolate sauce (page 24)
and vanilla ice cream.

chocolate-glazed cashew butter & cinnamon pie
Prepare basic recipe, substituting another nut butter (crunchy or smooth)
such as cashew for the peanut butter. Hazelnut, pecan or macadamia butters
would be equally good.

chocolate-glazed peanut butter pie with ginger crust
Prepare basic recipe, replacing chocolate crust with gingersnap crust.

milk chocolate-glazed peanut butter & cinnamon pie
Prepare basic recipe, topping the pie with a sweeter, less densely flavoured
topping by substituting good-quality milk chocolate for the dark.

chocolate-glazed peanut butter & cardamom pie
Prepare the basic recipe, replacing cinnamon in filling with ½ teaspoon
ground cardamom.

variations

apricot & pistachio tarte tatin

see base recipe page 92

apricot tarte tatin with shortcrust pastry
Prepare basic recipe, using a sweet shortcrust pastry instead of puff pastry (page 84).

apple tarte tatin
Prepare basic recipe, replacing apricots with apples, peeled, cored and thickly sliced. Pears would also work well.

apricot & almond tarte tatin
Prepare basic recipe, replacing pistachios with toasted flaked almonds (or chopped toasted pecans).

spicy apricot tarte tatin
Prepare basic recipe, adding 1 teaspoon ground cinnamon or ground ginger to the sugar and butter mixture.

mixed fruit tarte tatin
Prepare basic recipe, using a mix of different fruits rather than just apricots. Apples with blackberries tucked between, mango with sliced banana and halved plums and stoned cherries all work well.

plum frangipane tarts

see base recipe page 95

apricot frangipane tarts
Prepare basic recipe, substituting apricot jam for plum jam and apricots
for plums.

plum frangipane puff tarts
Prepare basic recipe, using 275 grams (10 ounces) thinly rolled puff pastry
instead of shortcrust.

plum & hazelnut frangipane tarts
Prepare basic recipe, replacing ground almonds in filling with ground
hazelnuts.

plum & cinnamon frangipane tarts
Prepare basic recipe, replacing grated lemon rind in filling with 1 teaspoon
ground cinnamon.

plum & sunflower seed frangipane tarts
Prepare basic recipe, scattering 2 tablespoons sunflower seeds over the
glazed tarts.

variations

cherry & custard filo tarts

see base recipe page 96

cherry & custard cream filo tarts
Prepare basic recipe, making custard with single cream or half cream and half milk instead of crème fraîche.

cherry & almond custard filo tarts
Prepare basic recipe, replacing vanilla essence in custard with almond flavouring.

cherry & custard puff tarts
Prepare basic recipe, replacing filo with about 250 grams (9 ounces) puff or shortcrust pastry. Roll out pastry thinly and line into individual, fairly deep, flan tins. Bake blind (using baking beans) until crisp and golden brown.

blueberry & custard filo tarts
Prepare basic recipe, replacing cherries in topping with blueberries or blackberries.

cherry & chocolate custard filo tarts
Prepare basic recipe, heating 55 grams (2 ounces) chopped or grated plain chocolate with crème fraîche until chocolate melts and crème fraîche comes to the boil.

french apple tart

see base recipe page 99

french apple tart with puff crust
Prepare basic recipe, replacing pastry with 350 grams (12 ounces) thinly rolled puff pastry.

spice-glazed french apple tart
Prepare basic recipe, replacing cinnamon in filling with ¼ teaspoon ground cloves or ground nutmeg.

french apple tart with almond pastry
Prepare basic recipe, replacing 55 grams (2 ounces) plain flour in pastry with same quantity of ground almonds.

french apple tart with apple compote
Prepare basic recipe, simmering 500 grams (1 pound) peeled, cored and chopped cooking apples with 3 tablespoons orange juice. Mash, then sweeten apple compote with a little caster sugar to taste before spooning into pastry case and topping with sliced apples.

french apple tart with pecans
Prepare basic recipe, scattering 2 tablespoons chopped pecans over the glazed tart.

variations

kiwi, orange & white chocolate mille-feuilles

see base recipe page 100

kiwi, orange & plain chocolate mille-feuilles
Prepare basic recipe, replacing white chocolate with dark chocolate.

seared kiwi, orange & white chocolate party mille-feuille
Prepare basic recipe, dividing puff pastry into 3 equal blocks and rolling out
each thinly to rectangles roughly 10 x 25 cm (4 x 10 inches). Bake until
golden brown without dusting with icing sugar. When cool, dust one layer
thickly with icing sugar, heat a metal skewer until very hot and mark a
crisscross pattern in the sugar, reheating skewer as necessary. This will be the
top layer. Stack the rectangles as in basic recipe, making 1 large mille-feuille.

kiwi, orange & plain chocolate mille-feuilles with hazelnuts
Prepare basic recipe, drizzling melted plain chocolate over top pieces of
pastry before assembling. Scatter over chopped toasted hazelnuts to serve.

kiwi & orange mille-feuilles with vanilla cream
Prepare basic recipe,
omitting white chocolate and using 250ml (8 fl oz) double cream, whipped
with 1 teaspoon vanilla essence.

mixed fresh fruit mille-feuilles
Prepare basic recipe, using mixed fruits in filling.

blackberry & apple oatmeal crumble

see base recipe page 102

blackberry, banana & apple oatmeal crumble
Prepare basic recipe, replacing 225 grams (8 ounces) apples with 2 medium bananas or 1 large one, peeled and sliced. Stir banana into cooked apples with the blackberries.

blackberry & apple crumble with almond topping
For a less crunchy topping, replace chopped walnuts with ground almonds.

mixed summer fruit oatmeal crumble
Prepare basic recipe, replacing blackberries with mixed fruits such as stoned cherries, raspberries and blueberries.

blackberry & apple crumble with muesli topping
Prepare basic recipe, replacing walnuts and oatmeal in topping with muesli.

blackberry & apple oatmeal–raisin crumble
Prepare basic recipe, replacing half the walnuts in topping with raisins.

meringues & choux pastry desserts

Stunning additions to a buffet party table and guaranteed to draw gasps of delight from your guests every time – nothing can beat a crisp, cloudlike meringue or pile of cream-filled profiteroles when you're cooking to impress.

meringue gâteau with lemon curd filling

see variations page 129

Meringues make delicious desserts, but unless you're into whipping up your own mayonnaise or crème anglaise, it can be a problem working out what to do with the egg yolks. In this recipe, the yolks are turned into lemon curd for the filling.

for the meringue
4 large egg whites
150 g (5½ oz) granulated sugar
85 g (3 oz) icing sugar
1 tbsp cornflour

for the lemon curd
finely grated rind and juice of 4 lemons
4 large egg yolks
110 g (4 oz) unsalted butter, cut up
225 g (8 oz) granulated sugar
extra icing sugar, to dust

Draw two 18-cm (7-inch) squares on two sheets of baking parchment. Place sheets upside down on baking trays. Preheat oven to 110°C (225°F/gas mark ¼). To make meringue, whisk egg whites until soft peak stage. Whisk in granulated sugar, a spoonful at a time, until mixture starts to thicken, then whisk in the rest in a slow, steady stream, continuing to whisk until thick and stiff. Sieve in icing sugar and cornflour and fold in gently with a large metal spoon until just combined. Pipe or spread the meringue over the drawn squares on the baking parchment. Bake for about 3 hours until dry and crisp. Cool in the turned-off oven. To make lemon curd, whisk rind, juice, yolks, butter and sugar in a large heatproof bowl. Place bowl over a pan of simmering water, and stir constantly until melted and thickened. Remove bowl from heat and cool, stirring occasionally. Chill until needed. Sandwich meringue layers with lemon curd and dust top with icing sugar. Serve with fruit.
Serves 8

mango meringue pie

see variations page 130

Traditional lemon meringue pie is given an exotic new twist with a tangy layer of fragrant mango under the puffy white cloud of meringue.

for the pastry
200 g (7 oz) plain flour
100 g (3½ oz) unsalted butter, cut up
2–3 tbsp chilled water
1 egg yolk

for the filling
2 very ripe mangoes
finely grated rind of 2 limes or 1 orange
for the topping
3 large egg whites
175 g (6 oz) caster sugar

To make the pastry, sieve flour into a bowl and rub in butter until the consistency is like breadcrumbs. Mix in enough chilled water to make a smooth, soft dough. Wrap dough in clingfilm and chill for 30 minutes.

Preheat oven to 190°C (375°F/gas mark 5). Roll out pastry on a lightly floured surface and line an 20-cm (8-inch) flan tin, about 3-cm (1¼ inches) deep. Line pastry with waxed paper, fill with baking beans and bake for 20 minutes. Remove beans and paper, brush base and sides of pastry with egg yolk and return to oven for 5 minutes. Remove from oven and allow to cool. Reduce oven temperature to 140°C (300°F/gas mark 2). To make the filling, peel, stone and chop mangoes. Mix with rind and spoon into pastry shell. To make the topping, whisk egg whites until standing in soft peaks, then whisk in sugar, a tablespoon at a time, until whites are stiff and shiny. Spoon meringue over chopped mango, carefully spreading it right to the edges so it forms a seal with pastry. Bake for 30 minutes or until meringue is golden and crisp. Allow to cool before serving.
Serves 6–8

cinnamon meringue slice layered with Caribbean fruits

see variations page 131

The meringue layers can be made ahead and stored in an airtight container and then assembled with the cream and fruit about 1-2 hours before serving.

for the meringue layers
3 large egg whites
55 g (2 oz) light brown sugar
110 g (4 oz) granulated sugar
1½ tsp cornflour
1½ tsp white wine vinegar
1 tsp ground cinnamon

for the filling
250 ml (8 fl oz) double cream
4 tbsp coconut milk
about 450 g (1 lb) mixed tropical fruits (such as papaya, figs, Cape gooseberries), prepared as necessary and cut into pieces

Preheat oven to 110°C (225°F/gas mark ¼). Draw two rectangles measuring 10x28 cm (4x11 inches) on a sheet of baking parchment. Place paper upside down on a baking tray. To make the meringue layers, whisk egg whites until standing in soft peaks. Whisk in brown sugar, a couple of teaspoonfuls at a time, so it is evenly incorporated. Then whisk in granulated sugar in three equal batches, adding cornflour, vinegar and cinnamon with final batch. Pipe or spread meringue over the marked rectangles, dividing it equally. Bake for 2–2½ hours or until pale golden and crisp. Let meringues cool in turned-off oven. When cooled completely, store in an airtight container. One or two hours before serving, make the filling. Whip cream and coconut milk together until stiff. Spread some coconut cream over one meringue layer and top with half the fruit. Top with more cream and put second meringue layer on top. Pipe or spoon remaining cream down the centre and decorate with remaining fruit. Chill until ready to serve. To serve, cut into slices with a sharp serrated knife.
Serves 6

strawberry, kiwi & orange pavlova

see variations page 132

A favourite party dessert that will never fail to elicit whoops of delight from your guests. Once you've whisked up the egg white mixture for the meringue, dab tiny blobs of it in each corner of the baking tray to stop the baking parchment sliding.

for the meringue
225g (8 oz) granulated sugar
1 tsp lemon juice
4 large egg whites
1 tbsp cornflour

for the filling
200 ml (7 oz) double cream
125 ml (4 fl oz) soured cream
finely grated rind of 1 orange
250 g (9 oz) fresh strawberries, sliced
1 orange, peeled and segmented
2 kiwi fruit, peeled and sliced

Draw a 23-cm (9-inch) circle on a sheet of baking parchment, turn parchment over and place it on a baking tray. Preheat oven to 140°C (275°F/gas mark 2). To make the meringue, put sugar, lemon juice and 1 egg white in a large bowl. Whisk with electric mixer on low speed until combined. Add another egg white, whisk for 2 minutes, then add remaining 2 whites and whisk for about 5 minutes on fast speed or until mixture is stiff and shiny. Finally, whisk in cornflour. Spoon meringue onto parchment. Spread it out to fill the drawn circle, hollowing out the centre a little. Bake for 1-1½ hours or until very pale golden and crisp on the outside but still soft in the middle. Turn off oven and leave meringue inside until it has cooled completely. No more than 1 hour before serving, make the filling. Whip cream, soured cream and orange rind together until mixture just holds its shape. Place meringue on a serving plate and spoon cream over it, leaving a narrow border around the top. Pile sliced strawberries, orange segments and kiwi slices over cream and serve.
Serves 6-8

choux ring with strawberries & blueberries

see variations page 133

You can pipe the choux onto the baking parchment or simply shape it with two spoons, but make sure the individual puffs are butted up close against each other.

for the choux ring
250 ml (8 fl oz) water
85 g (3 oz) unsalted butter, cut up
125 g (4½ oz) white bread flour, sieved
3 medium eggs, beaten
1 tbsp granulated sugar

for the filling
55 g (2 oz) granulated sugar
350 ml (12 fl oz) double cream
110 g (4 oz) fresh strawberries,
    hulled and sliced
110 g (4 oz) fresh blueberries
icing sugar, to dust

Preheat oven to 200°C (400°F/gas mark 6). Draw a 18-cm (7-inch) circle on a sheet of baking parchment and place it upside down on a greased baking tray. To make the choux ring, heat water and butter in a pan until melted. Bring to the boil, remove from heat and add flour. Beat briskly until mixture forms a smooth ball. Allow to cool slightly. Gradually beat in eggs, add the sugar with the last addition of egg. Not all the egg may be needed (although the paste should be smooth and shiny, it must still hold its shape). Spoon or pipe mixture into mounds around the marked circle. Bake for 40 minutes or until golden brown. Remove, carefully split the ring in half horizontally. Place halves split-side up on baking tray and return to oven for 5 minutes. Cool on a wire rack. To make the filling, whip sugar and cream together until it just holds its shape. If the choux ring has become soft, recrisp it in a hot oven. Spoon half the whipped cream over the bottom half of the cold choux ring; top with berries and remaining cream. Set lid on top and dust with icing sugar.

Serves 8–10

coffee meringue kisses

see variations page 134

These would make an attractive accompaniment to a bowl of fresh fruit or, if you decide not to serve a formal dessert, you could make mini versions and enjoy them with coffee or tea. The unfilled meringues can be made well ahead and stored in an airtight container.

for the meringues
3 large egg whites
175 g (6 oz) caster sugar
1 tsp coffee essence (or 1 tbsp instant coffee
    dissolved in 1 tbsp boiling water and cooled)

for the decoration & filling
175 g 6 oz plain chocolate, chopped
125 ml (4 fl oz) double cream
1 tsp vanilla essence
cocoa powder, to dust

Preheat oven to 110°C (225°F/gas mark ¼). Line two baking trays with baking parchment. To make the meringues, whisk egg whites in a large bowl until soft peak stage. Whisk in sugar, 1 teaspoon at a time to begin with. Then, as egg whites start to thicken, add sugar in a steady stream. When all the sugar has been added, whisk in coffee. Spoon or pipe 12 meringues on each baking tray. Bake for 2 hours or until dry and crisp. Cool in the turned-off oven, then carefully lift meringues from parchment.

To decorate and make the filling, melt chocolate in a bowl set over a pan of hot water, stirring occasionally until smooth. Line baking trays with clean parchment and dip bottoms of meringues in melted chocolate. Place them, chocolate-side down, on the parchment. Drizzle with remaining chocolate and allow to set. Whip cream with vanilla until it holds its shape. Use it to sandwich meringues together in pairs. Dust lightly with cocoa powder to serve.

Serves 12

almond & apricot meringue roulade

see variations page 135

Adding cornflour and either lemon juice or vinegar to the mixture keeps the centre of the baked meringue marshmallow-soft and the outside crisp.

for the roulade
4 large egg whites
150 g (5½ oz) granulated sugar, plus extra for dusting
2 tsp cornflour
1 tsp white wine vinegar or lemon juice
85 g (3 oz) blanched almonds, toasted and finely chopped to a coarse powder

for the filling
200 ml (7 fl oz) crème fraîche
300 g (11 oz) fresh or canned apricot halves, chopped
icing sugar, to dust

Grease and line a 23x33-cm (9x13-inch) Swiss roll tin with baking parchment. Preheat oven to 150°C (325°F/gas mark 3). For the roulade, whisk egg whites to soft peaks. Gradually whisk in sugar until mixture is stiff and shiny. Add cornflour and vinegar or lemon juice. Reserve 2 tablespoons almonds and fold the rest into meringue with a metal spoon. Spoon into prepared tin and spread out evenly to edges and corners. Scatter remaining almonds on top and bake for 25 minutes until pale golden. Lay a sheet of parchment on work surface and dust it with granulated sugar. Turn out meringue onto parchment, peel off lining paper and cool. To make the filling, spread crème fraîche over meringue, smoothing it out to the edges but leaving a border down one long side. Scatter chopped apricots over crème fraîche and roll up from the long side where the cream has been spread right to the edge. Place roulade on a serving plate, seam down and chill for 30 minutes. Dust with icing sugar to serve.
Serves 6–8

crackle-topped profiteroles with orange cream

see variations page 136

If the choux balls go soft when cool, put them back on a baking tray and return them to a hot oven for 5 minutes, which will recrisp them beautifully.

for the choux
80 g (3 oz) white bread flour
125 g (4 fl oz) water
55 g (2 oz) unsalted butter, in small pieces
2 medium eggs, beaten
1 tsp caster sugar
finely grated rind of 1 small orange

for the caramel
175 g (6 oz) granulated sugar
3 tbsp water
for the filling
grated rind from 1 orange and segments
    from 2 oranges
200 ml (7 fl oz) double or whipping cream

Preheat oven to 200°C (400°F/gas mark 6). Grease 2 baking trays and line with baking parchment. To make the choux, sieve flour onto a plate. Heat water and butter together in a pan over a low heat until butter has melted. Bring to the boil, remove from heat and add the flour. Beat with a wooden spoon until mixture forms a smooth ball. Allow to cool a little, then beat in eggs, a little at a time, with the sugar. Pipe 18 small balls, well spaced, onto the baking trays. Bake for 25 minutes, until crisp. Remove, pierce a hole in the side of each puff and return to oven for 5 minutes. Cool puffs on a wire rack. To make the caramel, heat sugar and water and boil until sugar caramelises and turns golden brown. Remove pan from heat and dip base of pan in cold water. Using tongs, dip top of each puff into caramel and set on a plate to cool and harden. remelt caramel over low heat if necessary. For the filling, place half the orange rind into a bowl, add cream and whip. Split profiteroles and fill with the cream and orange segments to serve.

Serves 6

floating islands with passion fruit crème anglaise

see variations page 137

Warming the passion fruit seeds and pulp makes it easier to separate them, but if you don't object to the seeds, simply stir the seeds and pulp into the crème anglaise.

for the crème anglaise
3 passion fruit
4 large egg yolks
55 g (2 oz) caster sugar
250 ml (8 fl oz) single cream

for the floating islands
2 large egg whites
110 g (4 oz) caster sugar
for the caramel
100 g (3½ oz) granulated sugar
2 tbsp water
3 tbsp toasted flaked almonds

To make crème anglaise, halve passion fruit and scoop seeds into a small bowl. Microwave for 30 seconds on full power, then strain to remove seeds. Whisk yolks and sugar together until pale and creamy. Heat cream until almost boiling. Stir cream into yolk mixture then return to pan. Stir over low heat without boiling until mixture coats the back of the spoon. Stir in passion fruit. To make floating islands, whisk egg whites to soft peaks. Gradually whisk in caster sugar until mixture is stiff and shiny. Half-fill a deep-frying pan with water and bring to a simmer. Spoon 6 small rounds of meringue into water and simmer over low heat for 2 minutes until they have doubled in size and feel firm, turning over once. Lift out meringues with a slotted spoon and drain on kitchen paper. Repeat with remaining mixture. To make caramel, dissolve sugar with water in a heavy pan and boil to a golden brown. Serve crème anglaise with meringues on top. Drizzle with hot caramel and sprinkle with almonds.
Serves 6

variations

meringue gâteau with lemon curd filling

see base recipe page 113

brown sugar meringue gâteau with lemon curd

Prepare basic recipe for meringue, substituting light brown sugar for granulated sugar and slowly whisking, rather than folding it in.

meringue gâteau with orange curd

Prepare basic recipe for lemon curd, replacing lemons with 2–3 oranges (depending on size). Or use 6 limes for lime curd.

meringue gâteau with fresh fruits & lemon curd

Prepare basic recipe, topping lemon curd with fresh fruit such as chopped peaches or strawberries, with passion fruit seeds and pulp spooned over, before adding top layer of meringue.

hazelnut meringue gâteau with lemon curd

Prepare basic recipe for meringue, folding in 2 tablespoons chopped hazelnuts at the end.

chocolate cream meringue gâteau

Prepare basic recipe, replacing lemon curd with chocolate cream. Melt 100 grams (3½ ounces) plain chocolate. Remove bowl from heat and stir in 125 ml (4 fl oz) crème fraîche. Allow to cool. Spread over meringue layer, top with raspberries and kiwi fruit slices and add second layer.

variations

mango meringue pie

see base recipe page 114

mango meringue pie with cinnamon crumb crust
Prepare basic recipe, replacing pastry with a spicy digestive biscuit crust. Add ½ teaspoon mixed spice and 1 teaspoon ground cinnamon to biscuit mixture. Press over base and sides of flan tin and chill while preparing the filling.

peach meringue pie
Prepare basic recipe, replacing mangoes with 4–5 peeled and stoned ripe peaches (depending on size). Nectarines also work well.

mango chocolate chip meringue pie
Prepare basic meringue recipe, folding 100 grams (3½ ounces) small plain chocolate chips or finely chopped plain chocolate into whisked egg whites.

mango & ginger meringue pie
Prepare basic recipe, adding 1 tablespoon preserved ginger to mango flesh.

apple meringue pie
Prepare basic recipe, replacing mangoes with 4–5 apples. Peel, core and chop apples and simmer with the lime rind and juice and 3 tablespoons water until softened. Purée apples and their cooking juices before cooling and spooning into pastry shell.

cinnamon meringue slice layered with Caribbean fruits

see base recipe page 117

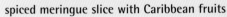

spiced meringue slice with Caribbean fruits
Prepare basic meringue, using only 225 grams (8 ounces) granulated sugar.
Replace cinnamon with ¼ teaspoon grated nutmeg and ¾ teaspoon mixed spice.

cinnamon meringue slice with orange cream
For filling, mix 2 tablespoons cornflour with 1 tablespoon water. Stir in 4 large
egg yolks, 100 grams (3½ ounces) caster sugar and grated rind and juice of
2 oranges. Bring 125 ml (4 fl oz) milk to the boil, pour onto yolk mixture, then
whisk until thick., cool, then fold in 125 ml (4 fl oz) cream, whipped.

Christmas meringue slice
For a spectacular Christmas dessert, prepare basic recipe, using chestnut cream
and winter fruits. Whip cream with 2 tablespoons chestnut purée and use fruits
such as tangerine segments, figs and poached cranberries.

pecan meringue slice with Caribbean fruits
Prepare basic recipe, folding 1 ounce coarsely ground pecans into meringue.

lemon mascarpone-filled meringue slice with Caribbean fruits
Prepare basic recipe, replacing filling with 250 grams (9 ounces) mascarpone
flavoured with grated rind and juice of 2 lemons.

strawberry, kiwi & orange pavlova

see base recipe page 118

chocolate-drizzled strawberry, kiwi & orange pavlova
Prepare basic recipe, drizzling baked meringue with 55 grams (2 ounces) each of melted plain chocolate and melted milk chocolate before filling.

golden fruits pavlova with coffee cream
Prepare basic recipe, replacing orange rind with 1 teaspoon coffee essence. Top with golden fruits, such as peaches or apricots and flaked almonds.

boozy strawberry & orange pavlova
Prepare basic recipe. Hull 500 grams (1 pound) small strawberries, and macerate in 2 tablespoons fruit liqueur for 30 minutes. Fold three-quarters of strawberries into filling. Top with remaining strawberries.

pretty-in-pink pavlova
Prepare basic recipe, adding a few drops of red food colouring to meringue mixture. Tint whipped cream, if you want and top with fruits to match – strawberries and raspberries.

individual fruit & ice cream pavlovas
Prepare basic recipe, making individual pavlovas and filling with ice cream and fruit.

variations

choux ring with strawberries & blueberries

see base recipe page 121

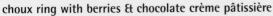

choux ring with berries & chocolate crème pâtissière
Prepare basic recipe, replacing whipped cream filling with chocolate crème pâtissière. Heat 250 ml (8 fl oz) whole milk with 25 grams (1 ounce) chopped plain chocolate until melted. Beat 2 large egg yolks with 55 grams (2 ounces) light brown sugar until creamy, stir in 2 tablespoons flour, then whisk in chocolate milk. Return to pan and stir over low heat until thickened. Dust top with sugar, cool and stir before using.

choux ring with lemon cream & lavender icing
Prepare basic recipe, adding finely grated rind of 1 lemon to whipping cream. Heat the juice of the lemon with 1 teaspoon culinary lavender, let stand for 30 minutes, then strain. Stir enough of the lavender-lemon juice into 150 grams (5½ ounces) icing sugar with a little violet food colouring and spread over the ring. Decorate with sprigs of lavender and a mixture of berries.

choux ring with berries & white chocolate drizzle
Prepare basic recipe, drizzling filled ring with 85 grams (3 ounces) melted white chocolate.

chocolate choux ring with berries
Prepare basic recipe for choux, replacing 1 tablespoon flour with 1 tablespoon cocoa powder.

variations

coffee meringue kisses

see base recipe page 122

coconut meringue kisses
Prepare basic recipe, omitting coffee flavouring from meringues and
chocolate from whipped cream. Brush tops of cooked meringues with
warmed apricot or strawberry jam and coat them in toasted flaked coconut.
Sandwich in pairs with whipped cream and strawberry or apricot slices.

mocha hazelnut meringue kisses
Prepare basic recipe, dipping bases of the meringues first in melted plain
chocolate and then in chopped toasted hazelnuts.

choc-n-orange meringue kisses with peppermint cream
Prepare basic recipe. Omit coffee flavouring and fold in 85 grams (3 ounces)
finely chopped orange-flavoured dark chocolate. Sandwich meringues with
whipped cream flavoured with 1 teaspoon peppermint essence instead
of vanilla.

rainbow meringue kisses
Prepare basic recipe, replacing plain chocolate with white chocolate and tint
with a few drops of food colouring of choice. To serve scatter with sprinkles.

coffee & almond meringue kisses
Prepare recipe, folding 2 tablespoons ground almonds in meringue mixture.

almond & apricot meringue roulade

see base recipe page 124

raspberry & rosewater meringue roulade
Prepare basic recipe, adding 1 teaspoon rosewater to both the roulade mixture and the crème fraîche. Replace apricots with 250 grams (9 ounces) lightly crushed raspberries and the seeds of 1 pomegranate. Scatter crystallised rose petals over to serve.

macadamia & apricot meringue roulade
Prepare basic recipe, replacing ground almonds with toasted and coarsely ground macadamia nuts (or pecans).

peach & orange meringue roulade
Prepare basic recipe, adding finely grated rind of 1 orange to meringue mixture and filling roulade with mix of orange and peach pieces instead of apricots.

blueberry, cherry & lemon meringue roulade
Prepare basic recipe, replacing ground almonds in roulade with the finely grated rind of 1 lemon. Replace apricots in filling with equal quantities of blueberries and stoned cherries.

strawberry, pineapple & mascarpone meringue roulade
Prepare basic recipe, replacing crème fraîche with mascarponeand apricots with equal quantities of chopped strawberries and pineapple pieces.

variations

crackle-topped profiteroles with orange cream

see base recipe page 127

orange cream profiteroles with plain chocolatesauce
Prepare basic recipe, omitting caramel. Serve with chocolate sauce (page 24).

orange cream choux pyramid with spun sugar
Prepare basic recipe, filling buns with orange cream by making a hole in the base and piping in the cream. Make the caramel with 250 grams (9 ounces) granulated sugar and 4 tablespoons water. Dip puffs into caramel and stack in a pyramid shape, sticking them together with the caramel. Return remaining caramel to heat, dip 2 forks in it and flick strands of sugar over buns, repeating until pyramid is covered with fine threads.

crackle-topped profiteroles with pistachios and orange cream
Prepare basic recipe, sprinkling tops with chopped pistachios.

crackle-topped profiteroles with chocolate cream
Prepare basic recipe, replacing orange cream with whipped cream flavoured with 1 tablespoon cocoa powder dissolved in 1 tablespoon hot water.

crackle-topped profiteroles filled with ice cream
Prepare basic recipe, replacing orange cream with small scoops of orange or another flavour of ice cream.

floating islands with passion fruit crème anglaise

see base recipe page 128

floating islands with raspberry crème anglaise
Prepare basic recipe, replacing passion fruit in crème anglaise with 110 grams
(4 ounces) puréed and strained raspberries. Serve scattered with whole raspberries.

floating islands with fresh fruit & crème anglaise
Prepare basic recipe, adding a layer of fruit such as chopped banana, mango,
sliced apricots or kiwi fruit.

floating islands with pomegranate & pistachios
Prepare basic recipe, replacing passion fruit with 1 tablespoon grenadine. Replace
almond topping with pomegranate seeds and chopped pistachios.

floating islands with chocolate crème anglaise
Prepare basic recipe, omitting passion fruit purée. Heat 55 grams (2 ounces)
grated or chopped plain chocolate with the cream, stirring until melted and use
only 3 egg yolks.

floating islands with light coffee crème anglaise
For a less rich crème anglaise, prepare basic recipe, replacing cream with whole
milk or mix of milk and cream. Instead of fruit purée, flavour crème anglaise with
1 teaspoon coffee essence or 2 tablespoons rum or brandy.

chilled desserts

From mastering the art of using gelatin to whipping

up a creamy zabaglione or caramelising a brulée,

you'll find all you need to know – and plenty more –

in this chapter of delicious desserts to make ahead

and chill in the fridge.

coconut panna cotta with passion fruit coulis

see variations page 160

In Italian, panna cotta simply means "cooked cream" and the soft, silky texture of this famous dessert makes it a lovely finale to a special meal. The creams can be set in individual moulds, turned out and the coulis spooned around or they can be served in glasses as they are here.

for the panna cotta
1 tbsp unflavoured gelatin
2 tbsp cold water
250 ml (8 fl oz) double cream
125 ml (4 fl oz) coconut milk

150 ml (5 fl oz) natural Greek yogurt
100 g (3½ oz) caster sugar
for the coulis
6 passion fruit, halved
350 ml (12 fl oz) freshly squeezed orange juice

To make the panna cotta, sprinkle gelatin over cold water and soak for 5 minutes. Then place the bowl in a pan of hot water, stirring until smooth and all granules have dissolved. Place cream, coconut milk, yogurt and sugar in a pan. Heat gently until sugar melts and bubbles appear on surface. Remove pan from heat and stir in dissolved gelatin. Cool a little, then pour mixture into 6 glass dishes. Chill for several hours or overnight until set.

To make the coulis, scoop out passion fruit seeds and pulp into a small pan. Add orange juice, bring to the boil and simmer for about 10 minutes until sauce reduces by about half. Push sauce through a sieve to remove seeds and allow to cool. Spoon coulis over panna cotta and chill until ready to serve.

Serves 6

rum & ricotta pudding

see variations page 161

One of the simplest desserts, this is a wonderful way to enjoy really fresh, good-quality ricotta. It is very soft in texture, which makes it perfect for dunking biscotti.

450 g (1 lb) ricotta
60 g (2½ oz) icing sugar, sieved
3 large egg yolks
4 tbsp dark rum

1 tbsp dessert wine such as Marsala or Vinsanto
250 ml (8 fl. oz) whipping cream, whipped
    until stiff

Mix together the ricotta, icing sugar and egg yolks until you have a thick creamy texture. Stir in the rum and dessert wine, then fold in the whipped cream. Serve in chilled stemmed glasses, with biscotti for dunking. You can make this in advance and keep chilled until required, or whip it together quickly at the last moment.

Serves 6

blueberry muffin trifles

see variations page 162

Chill these for an hour or so before serving – they can also be made the day before and kept in the fridge overnight. Use a custard powder to make the custard or use the recipe on pages 24–25.

4 blueberry muffins, cut into 15 mm (½-inch) pieces
250 ml (9 oz) fresh blackberries or blackcurrants
25 g (1 oz) caster sugar

125 ml (4 fl oz) orange juice
225 g (8 oz) fresh blueberries
500 ml (16 fl oz) cold thick custard
125 ml (4 fl oz) crème fraîche
25 g (1 oz) toasted flaked almonds

Divide muffins between 6 individual dishes or place in a large glass bowl. Put blackberries or blackcurrants in a pan, add sugar and orange juice and simmer over low heat until fruit has softened. Purée in a liquidiser or food processor and allow to cool before stirring in half the blueberries. Spoon all but 2 tablespoons of blueberry sauce over muffins.

Divide custard between dishes, spreading it in an even layer. Top with blobs of crème fraîche and remaining blueberry sauce. Scatter oover almonds and remaining blueberries. Refrigerate until ready to serve.

Serves 6

il montebianco

see variations page 163

I have adapted this recipe from the more complicated and long-winded version that ends up with a mountain of cream, chestnut puréeand chocolate on a large platter. You'll need a potato ricer or mouli food mill to make this version.

450 g (1 lb) tinned sweetened chestnut purée
4 tbsp Strega liqueur (optional)
700 ml (24 fl oz) double or whipping cream
2 tbsp sieved icing sugar
1 tsp vanilla essence
3 large ready-made meringues, crushed
85 g (3 oz) good-quality plain chocolate
    (minimum cocoa solids content 70%), grated

1 tbsp best-quality unsweetened powdered
    chocolate for dusting
1½ tbsp sieved icing sugar
    for dusting
6 marrons glacés and 12 crystallised violets,
    to garnish

Mash the chestnut purée as much as possible to soften it, then mix with Strega if using. Set aside until required. Whip the cream, then sweeten with icing sugar and flavour with vanilla essence. Fill the bottom of 6 glasses with a little crushed meringue and cover with a layer of whipped cream. Push chestnut purée through a ricer or food mill onto whipped cream, then sprinkle with grated chocolate. Add another layer of purée and cover with whipped cream and chocolate as before. Add another layer of crushed meringues, then cover with a final layer of whipped cream. Allow a final small amount of chestnut purée to fall over the whipped cream, then sieve the powdered chocolate and icing sugar, mixed together, on top to dust lightly. Chill until required. Garnish with marrons glacés and crystallised violets before serving.

Serves 6

mango & mascarpone brûlées

see variations page 164

It's important to pick out a ripe mango, because if it's still hard it will also be tasteless, and have no sweet aroma, resulting in a disappointing dessert rather than one that is lush and fragrant.

1 ripe mango
6 large egg yolks
55 g (2 oz) granulated sugar
110 g (4 oz) mascarpone cheese

350 ml (12 fl oz) single cream
½ tsp vanilla essence
4 tbsp light brown sugar

Peel mango and cut flesh away from stone. Chop flesh into small pieces or purée in food processor. Spoon into 6 medium-size ramekins or other heatproof dishes.

Beat together egg yolks and sugar until sugar has dissolved and mixture is light and creamy. Heat mascarpone and cream gently over low heat, stirring occasionally to combine, until bubbles begin to appear on surface. Pour onto yolk mixture, add vanilla and stir well to combine. Strain custard into ramekins and place them in a roasting tin. Pour hot water into pan to come about 2.5 cm (1 inch) up sides of ramekins.

Preheat oven to 140°C (300°F/gas mark 2). Bake custards for 30–35 minutes or until just set. Remove from roasting tin and allow to cool, then chill for several hours. About 1 hour before serving, spoon brown sugar evenly over custards, completely covering the top. Caramelise under grill or use a cook's blowtorch until sugar is a rich dark brown and crisp. Allow to cool so topping hardens.

Serves 6

tiramisu with pears

see variations page 165

A fruity variation on the Italian specialty that has become one of the world's favourite desserts. If you prefer, it can be made in one large dish, and if children are in the party, omit the liqueur.

110 g (4 oz) sponge fingers, coarsely chopped
125 ml (4 fl oz) cold strong black coffee
2 tbsp Tia Maria or Kahlua liqueur
1–2 ripe pears (depending on size), peeled,
   cored and chopped or sliced

85 g (3 oz) caster sugar
500 g (18 oz) mascarpone cheese
1 tsp unsweetened cocoa powder

Place some of the chopped sponge fingers in bottom of 4 dessert dishes. Mix coffee and liqueur together and spoon a little over sponge fingers.

Stir three-quarters of the pears into mascarpone with the sugar, then spoon a layer into each dish. Continue layering sponge fingers, coffee and mascarpone mixture in dishes, finishing with a mascarpone layer. Chill until ready to serve.

Just before serving top each tiramisu with a few pear slices and dust with cocoa.

Serves 4

cappuccino whips

see variations page 166

You can buy custard or make your own (pages 24–25) for these creamy treats. The custard should have the consistency of unwhipped double cream or what the French call crème anglaise.

125 ml (4 fl oz) double cream
250 ml 8 fl oz) pouring custard
2 tbsp espresso or strong black coffee

125 g (5½ oz) milk chocolate, chopped
extra whipped cream and grated plain
chocolate, to decorate

Heat cream, custard and coffee together until almost boiling. Remove pan from heat and add chopped chocolate, stirring until chocolate melts. Cool and leave until starting to thicken, stirring occasionally. Then, spoon into small cups or glasses and chill for 2–3 hours to firm. To serve, top with a spoonful of whipped cream and sprinkle with grated chocolate.

Serves 4

apricot, honey & ricotta mousse

see variations page 167

When they're in season, use fresh apricots rather than canned to make the mousse, topping off the liquid to make the gelatin with extra apple juice.

1 x 400-g (14½-oz) can apricot halves in fruit juice
2 tbsp honey
250 g (9 oz) ricotta cheese
125 ml (4 fl oz) double cream

1 package lemon jelly
to decorate
6 tbsp double cream or Greek yogurt
3 tbsp toasted chopped nuts
6 tsp honey

Drain apricot halves, reserving juice and two halves for decoration. Put remaining apricots in a food processor or liquidiser and add honey and ricotta. Blend together until smooth. In a large bowl, whip cream until thick. Add apricot mixture and stir until evenly mixed. Make the lemon jelly according to package instructions, but use only 350 ml (12 fl oz) liquid. Use enough boiling water to dissolve the jelly, then top off with juice from apricot can. Set aside until jelly starts to thicken. Gradually stir apricot mixture into thickened gelatin. Spoon into stemmed glasses or serving dishes and chill until set.

Decorate each mousse with a spoonful of double cream or Greek yogurt, a scattering of chopped nuts and chopped reserved apricot halves. Drizzle with honey.

Serves 6

rhubarb fool

see variations page 168

The slim young stalks of early rhubarb are vivid pink in colour, so they give desserts such as this creamy fool a real lift. Later rhubarb tends to be greener, so a dash of pink food colouring might be needed to provide the necessary eye appeal. You can make this in the morning and let it chill all day, if you like.

1 lb fresh rhubarb
110 g (4 oz) light brown sugar
juice of 1 lemon
1 tbsp custard powder

125 ml (4 fl oz) milk
pink food colouring (optional)
125 ml (4 fl oz) whipping cream
crushed gingersnaps, to decorate

Preheat oven to 180°C (350°F/gas mark 4). Cut rhubarb stalks into 5-cm (2-inch) lengths, place in a bowl and mix with sugar and lemon juice. Pour rhubarb into a shallow baking tin, spread out evenly and bake for 10 minutes. Allow to cool and then purée in a food processor or liquidiser.

Mix custard powder with a little milk. Heat remaining milk in a small pan until almost boiling, pour onto custard powder and stir until mixed. Return pan to low heat and stir until custard is smooth and thickened. Whisk custard into puréed rhubarb, add a little pink food colouring if necessary and allow to cool. Whip cream until standing in soft peaks. Fold three-quarters of the whipped cream into rhubarb custard and spoon into serving glasses or dishes. Divide remaining cream between dishes and swirl in with a skewer. Chill until ready to serve. Serve decorated with a sprinkling of crushed gingersnaps.

Serves 4

sparkling clementine jelly

see variations page 169

A pretty party dessert that's low in calories if you go easy on the cream or replace it with reduced-fat crème fraîche or yogurt.

1½ tbsp unflavoured gelatin
3 tbsp cold water
400 ml (13 fl oz) dry pink champagne or
    sparkling wine

few drops of pink food colouring (optional)
1 tbsp caster sugar
4 clementines
whipped cream, to serve

Soak gelatin in the cold water for 5 minutes to soften, then dissolve by placing the bowl in a pan of hot water. Pour about one-third of the champagne or sparkling wine into a small pan. Add gelatin and sugar, then heat gently until sugar dissolves. Remove from heat and pour into a measuring jug or small pitcher. Top off with remaining champagne or wine, adding a few drops of food colouring if desired.

Peel clementines, pull away any loose pith and with a sharp knife, slice a couple of pieces of rind into fine strips. Keep in a small bowl of cold water until needed. Divide half the clementine slices between 4 stemmed wine or cocktail glasses and pour in enough of the champagne mixture to cover them. Chill until just set, add remaining clementine slices (reserving a few for decoration) and then carefully pour remaining mixture into glasses. Chill again until firmly set. Top each jelly with a spoonful of whipped cream, reserved clementine slices and a few strips of rind.

Serves 4

orange zabaglione with chocolate cake pops

see variations page 170

Warm zabaglione is a delicious dessert, but it does involve lots of last minute whipping – time you'd probably rather spend chatting to your guests. This version can be made ahead and chilled until needed.

for the zabaglione
4 large egg yolks
finely grated rind of 2 oranges
100 g (3½ oz) granulated sugar
6½ tbsp Marsala
for the chocolate cake pops
100 g (3½ oz) plain sponge cake crumbs

2 tsp dark brown sugar
55 g (2 oz) plain chocolate, melted
55 g (2 oz) unsalted butter, melted
225 g (8 oz) milk or white chocolate, melted
chocolate sprinkles or other small
    edible decorations

To make the zabaglione, put egg yolks, half the orange rind and sugar in a large bowl and whisk together until foamy. Add Marsala and whisk again briefly. Set bowl over a pan of simmering water, making sure bottom of bowl doesn't touch water and whisk until mixture becomes very thick and creamy. Spoon into 4 dessert glasses or dishes and chill for at least 1 hour or until ready to serve. To make the chocolate cake pops, put cake crumbs in a bowl and stir in sugar, melted dark chocolate and butter. Knead mixture together and shape into 8 small balls. Chill until firm. Dip balls in melted milk or white chocolate, scatter chocolate sprinkles over them and put on a plate or baking tray lined with foil. Leave in a cool place (not the fridge) until chocolate has set. Push a plastic lollipop stick into each, making a small hole in the chocolate shell with the point of a sharp knife, if necessary. Serve with zabaglione.
Serves 4

mango & lime mousse

see variations page 171

Sweet, aromatic mangoes are a real taste of the tropics, but, as with all exotic fruits, it's good to use your nose before you buy. If a mango has a honeyed, fragrant aroma, the chances are it will taste good too. No scent usually means no flavour either.

1 tbsp unflavoured gelatin
2 tbsp cold water
2–3 mangoes (total weight of prepared flesh
    about 450 g (1 lb))
finely grated rind and juice of 2 limes

175 ml (6 fl oz) double cream
1 large egg white
55 g (2 oz) light brown sugar
extra whipped cream and shreds of lime rind,
    to decorate

In a small bowl, soak gelatin in the cold water for 5 minutes. Set bowl in a pan of hot water and leave until gelatin has dissolved.

Peel mangoes and cut flesh away from fibrous stone. Chop flesh coarsely and place in a food processor or liquidiser with lime rind and juice. Blend to a purée. Stir in dissolved gelatin.

Whip cream until it just holds its shape and fold into mango mixture. Whisk egg white until standing in soft peaks, then gradually whisk in sugar. Stir 1 tablespoon whisked egg white into mango mixture and then gently fold in the rest. Spoon into serving dishes and chill for 2–3 hours until set. Decorate each mousse with a spoonful of whipped cream and a few fine shreds of lime rind.

Serves 6

coconut panna cotta with passion fruit coulis

see base recipe page 139

orange panna cotta with passion fruit coulis
Prepare basic recipe, replacing coconut milk with whole milk and adding finely grated rind of 1 orange to cream mixture.

coconut panna cotta with mango coulis
Prepare basic recipe, replacing passion fruit coulis with mango coulis. Purée flesh of 1 ripe mango with enough exotic fruit juice to make smooth sauce.

chocolate panna cotta with passion fruit coulis
Prepare basic recipe, replacing coconut milk with single cream and adding 2 teaspoons cocoa powder, dissolved in 1 tablespoon hot water.

coffee panna cotta with crunchy hazelnut topping
Prepare basic recipe, replacing coconut milk with cold black coffee. Sprinkle chilled panna cotta with chopped toasted hazelnuts and chocolate-covered coffee beans.

berry smoothie panna cotta
Prepare basic recipe, replacing coconut milk with a strawberry or blueberry smoothie. Top with strawberry or blueberry coulis, made by puréeing 250 grams (9 ounces) strawberries or blueberries with enough apple or orange juice to make a smooth sauce, about 175 ml (6 fl oz).

variations

rum & ricotta pudding

see base recipe page 140

rum and ricotta pudding with toasted almonds
Prepare basic recipe, adding 3 tablespoons slivered toasted almonds along with the rum and dessert wine. Sprinkle the top of each serving with a few more almonds.

coffee ricotta pudding
Prepare basic recipe, replacing the dark rum with the same amount of strong espresso. Garnish each serving with a coffee bean

limoncello & ricotta pudding
Prepare basic recipe, adding the grated zest of 1 lemon and replacing the rum and dessert wine with 5 tablespoons limoncello liqueur.

amaretti & ricotta pudding
Prepare basic recipe, crumbling 6 amaretti biscuits into the mixture before folding in the whipped cream. Serve with amaretti biscuits for dunking.

variations

blueberry muffin trifles

see base recipe page 142

raspberry muffin trifles
Prepare basic recipe, using raspberry muffins and raspberries instead of blueberries. Replace blackberries or blackcurrants in purée with strawberries.

blueberry muffin trifles with vanilla sauce
Prepare basic recipe, replacing custard with vanilla cream sauce. Mix 3 large egg yolks with 85 grams (3 ounces) icing sugar, 1½ tablespoons cornflour and 2 tablespoons milk until smooth. Heat remaining milk with 125 ml (4 fl oz) single cream until almost boiling, whisk into egg mixture, then return to pan and stir over a low heat until thick and smooth. Stir in 1 teaspoon vanilla essence and cool before spooning over muffins and fruit purée.

blueberry muffin trifles with whipped cream & amaretti
Prepare basic recipe, topping trifles with spoonfuls of whipped cream and scattering crushed amaretti over them with the blueberries.

variations

il montebianco

see base recipe page 145

montebianco al cioccolato bianco
Prepare basic recipe, replacing the chocolate with grated white chocolate
and the powdered chocolate with melted white chocolate.

montebianco al gianduja
Prepare basic recipe, replacing the grated chocolate with grated gianduja
chocolate (a speciality chocolate from Turin containing hazelnuts) and the
powdered chocolate with melted gianduja.

montebianco al Strega
Prepare basic recipe, replacing the brandy with Strega liqueur.

variations

mango & mascarpone brûlées

see base recipe page 146

peach & mascarpone brûlées
Prepare basic recipe, replacing mango with 2–3 ripe peaches, depending on size, peeled and stoned.

mango & crème fraîche brûlées
Prepare basic recipe, replacing mascarpone with crème fraîche.

apricot, almond & mascarpone brûlées
Prepare basic recipe, replacing mango with 4 large stoned apricots, puréeing them with 2 tablespoons amaretto liqueur or a few drops of almond essence.

mango & chocolate brûlées
Prepare basic recipe, whisking 1 tablespoon cocoa powder, dissolved in 1 tablespoon hot water and cooled, with egg yolks and sugar.

blueberry brûlées
Prepare basic recipe, replacing mango with 175 grams (6 ounces) fresh blueberries, roughly chopped (not puréed) and divided between ramekins.

tiramisu with pears

see base recipe page 148

ginger tiramisu with pears
Prepare basic recipe, replacing sponge fingers with gingerbread, broken into small pieces.

tiramisu with nectarines
Prepare basic recipe, replacing pears with 1–2 nectarines, depending on size, stoned and chopped.

pear & orange tiramisu
Prepare basic recipe, stirring 1 teaspoon finely grated orange rind into mascarpone with chopped pears.

tiramisu with pears & grappa
Prepare basic recipe, replacing coffee liqueur with the Italian brandy, grappa.

tiramisu with grapes
Prepare basic recipe, replacing pears with 140 grams (5 ounces) seedless green grapes, halved or roughly chopped.

variations

cappuccino whips

see base recipe page 150

mocha whips
Prepare basic recipe, replacing milk chocolate with plain chocolate.

boozy cappuccino whips
Prepare basic recipe, stirring 2 tablespoons coffee liqueur into cream mixture after adding the chocolate.

white cappuccino whips
Prepare basic recipe, replacing milk chocolate with white chocolate and stirring in ½ teaspoon vanilla essence after chocolate has melted.

pear & cappuccino whips
Prepare basic recipe, adding a chopped pear half to each serving cup or glass before spooning in the whip.

orange cappuccino whips
Prepare basic recipe, adding 1 teaspoon finely grated orange rind to cream, custard and coffee mixture before heating.

variations

apricot, honey & ricotta mousse

see base recipe page 152

peach, honey & ricotta mousse
Prepare basic recipe, substituting 1 x 400-gram (14½-ounce) tin peach halves in fruit juice for apricots. Reserve only one peach half for decoration.

apricot, maple & ricotta mousse
Prepare basic recipe, replacing honey with 3 tablespoons maple syrup when making mousse and drizzling extra syrup over for decoration.

apricot, honey & yogurt mousse
Prepare basic recipe, replacing 110 grams (4 ounces) of ricotta with natural Greek yogurt.

apricotorange and ricotta mousse
Prepare basic recipe, replacing apple juice with orange juice.

apricot, honey & yogurt mousse with blueberry topping
Prepare basic recipe, replacing cream or yogurt topping with blueberry compote. Simmer 300 grams (11 ounces) blueberries with 125 ml (4 fl oz) orange juice in a covered pan until blueberries are soft. Mix 2 teaspoons arrowroot with 2 tablespoons cold water and stir into berries. Heat gently until sauce thickens, stirring occasionally. Allow to cool, then spoon some compote over each mousse.

variations

rhubarb fool

see base recipe page 153

blackberry fool
Prepare basic recipe, replacing rhubarb with 450 grams (1 pound)
blackberries and omitting lemon juice. Simmer blackberries with 125 ml
(4 fl oz) orange juice until soft, then blend in a food processor. Push mixture
through a sieve and discard seeds. Stir in 2 tablespoons light brown sugar.

plum & cardamom fool
Prepare basic recipe, replacing rhubarb with 700 grams (1½ pounds)
red plums, halved and stoned and adding 1 teaspoon ground cardamom
before baking.

rhubarb & yogurt fool
Prepare basic recipe, replacing whipping cream with natural Greek yogurt.

raspberry fool
Prepare basic recipe, replacing rhubarb with 350 grams (12 ounces)
raspberries. Crush lightly with a fork, sprinkle with 2 tablespoons light brown
sugar and the lemon juice and set aside. Fold raspberries into custard with
their juice, before adding whipped cream.

sparkling clementine jelly

see base recipe page 154

rosé clementine jellies
Prepare basic recipe, replacing pink champagne with a dry rosé wine such as one from Chile or the south of France.

sparkling apple & raspberry jellies
Prepare basic recipe, replacing pink champagne with clear sparkling apple juice and the clementines with 225 grams (8 ounces) raspberries. As apple juice is naturally sweet, the sugar can probably be omitted but taste the jelly if you're unsure.

port, cranberry & cherry jellies
Prepare basic recipe, replacing pink champagne with 85 ml (3 fl oz) ruby port and 250 ml (8 fl oz) cranberry juice (or use all cranberry juice) and the clementines with 225 grams (8 ounces) stoned black or red cherries.

sparkling bellini jellies
Prepare basic recipe, replacing pink champagne with Italian Prosecco (sparkling wine) and clementines with 2 ripe peaches, peeled, stoned, and chopped.

variations

orange zabaglione with chocolate cake pops

see base recipe page 156

orange zabaglione with chocolate drizzle
Prepare basic recipe, omitting cake pops. Melt 100 grams (3½ ounces) plain chocolate with 4 tablespoons double cream. Cool and drizzle over zabaglione to serve.

orange zabaglione with orange slices & caramelised orange rind
Prepare basic recipe. Peel 2 large oranges, cut away pith and divide into segments. Place in glasses before adding zabaglione. Decorate each glass with caramelised orange rind. Simmer fine strips of rind in a sugar syrup made with 125 ml (4 fl oz) water and 110 grams (4 oz) icing sugar for 10 minutes until syrup reduces by about half. Cool zest in syrup.

warm orange zabaglione with chocolate cake pops
Prepare basic recipe, serving zabaglione immediately while still warm.

orange zabaglione with ginger cake pops
Prepare basic recipe, replacing plain sponge cake crumbs with gingerbreadcrumbs in the cake pops.

lemon zabaglione with chocolate cake pops
Prepare basic recipe, replacing orange rind with the rind of 2 lemons.

mango & lime mousse

see base recipe page 158

lychee & strawberry mousse
Prepare basic recipe, replacing mangoes with 450 grams (1 pound) peeled and
stoned lychees and hulled strawberries (prepared total weight).

peach & orange mousse
Prepare basic recipe, replacing mangoes with 450 grams (1 pound) peeled and
stoned peaches (prepared weight). Replace lime rind and juice with grated rind
and juice of 1 small orange.

mango & rum mousse
Prepare basic recipe, adding 2 tablespoons white or gold rum to whipped cream.

mango & coconut mousse
Prepare basic recipe, replacing cream with thick coconut milk (no need to whip it)
and folding this into the mango mixture.

mango & ginger mousse
Prepare basic recipe, sprinkling the top of each mousse with crushed gingersnaps.

frozen treats

A sophisticated strawberry semifreddo, creamy and tangy limoncello ice cream, exotic coconut Malibu Alaska and a palate-cleansing pomegranate and lychee granita are just a few of the frozen delights you'll find in this chapter.

strawberry semifreddo

see variations page 194

An impressive but easy dessert that tastes as good as it looks. As vanilla is quite sweet, the sharp flavor of the strawberries provides a good contrast.

500 g stawberries
3 eggs
2 egg yolks
1 tsp. vanilla extract
200 g caster sugar

400 ml cream
25g icing sugar
2 tsp. lemon juice
redcurrants, to decorate

Line a 13 x 23cm loaf tin with cling film. Reserve 2 strawberries for the decoration. Crush the remaining strawberries with a potato masher to make a chunky puree. Put the eggs, egg yolks, vanilla and caster sugar in a heatproof bowl, place over a pan of simmering (not boiling) water and whisk with an electric whisk for 4 minutes. Remove from the heat and whisk until thick, frothy and completely cool. Whisk the cream until thick and fold into the egg mixture. Spoon the mixture into the tin. Drizzle over half the strawberry puree and pass the handle of a wooden spoon through the mixture to produce a lightly marbled effect. Smooth the surface, cover with cling film and freeze for at least 6 hours or overnight if possible.

Press the remaining puree through a fine sieve into a bowl. Stir in the icing sugar and lemon juice. Turn the semifreddo out of the tin on to a serving plate and peel away the cling film. Drizzle with a little strawberry puree. Put the remaining strawberry puree into a small bowl. Decorate with redcurrants and the reserved strawberries. Cut into slices using a warmed knife and serve drizzled with strawberry puree.

Serves 6

coconut malibu alaska

see variations page 195

Store-bought vanilla ice cream can be used to make this crunchy-topped dessert if you prefer, but choose a good-quality one that isn't soft scoop, which would melt too quickly in the oven.

750 ml (1 ¼ pints) vanilla ice cream
1 large ripe mango or small papaya, peeled
    and chopped
2 tbsp Malibu coconut liqueur

4 egg whites
175 ml (6 oz) caster sugar
225 g (8 oz) gingerbread, sliced
2 tbsp unsweetened flaked coconut

Line a 1-kg (2-lb) loaf tin with a double thickness of clingfilm, letting it overhang the sides. Spoon ice cream into tin, packing it down firmly and hollowing out the middle. Purée the mango or papaya with the coconut liqueur and spoon into hollow. Fold clingfilm over the top to cover and return to freezer until ready to serve. Before serving, preheat oven to its hottest setting. Whisk egg whites until standing in soft peaks, then gradually whisk in sugar until stiff.

Peel back clingfilm from mango and ice cream and cover the top with gingerbread slices, pressing them down lightly. Invert onto a baking tray and unmould. Pull off clingfilm and cover dessert with the meringue, spreading it over top and sides with a palette knife and creating a seal around the bottom. Sprinkle with coconut and bake for 5 minutes or until golden brown. Serve at once, cut into slices.

Serves 6

blackberry & mint parfait with amaretti

see variations page 196

Mint is a deliciously refreshing herb and one of the most versatile, as it's equally at home in savoury dishes as sweet dishes. In this creamy parfait, it partners with blackberries to make a lovely summertime dessert. You can make your own sauce by using the recipe for raspberry coulis (page 24) and substituting blackberries for the raspberries or buy a ready-made blackberry sauce.

350 g (12 oz) fresh blackberries
6 fresh mint leaves, roughly torn
110 g (4 oz) icing sugar
1 tbsp lemon juice
250 ml (8 oz) double cream

125 ml (4 fl oz) single cream
110 g (4 oz) amaretti biscuits, crushed
blackberry dessert sauce, to serve
extra blackberries and mint leaves, to serve

Purée blackberries in a food processor or liquidiser with mint leaves, icing sugar and lemon juice. In a bowl, whip creams together until thick, then fold in blackberry purée. Spoon into eight 125-ml (4-fl oz) cups or moulds (you could use empty yogurt containers), cover tops with foil and freeze until solid. Transfer parfaits to fridge about 20 minutes before serving. Turn out onto serving plates and sprinkle with crushed amaretti. Serve with blackberry dessert sauce and garnish with extra blackberries and mint leaves.

Serves 8

brown bread & hazelnut ice cream

see variations page 197

An excellent recipe for using up leftover bread. The ice cream can be served on its own or with fresh fruit such as strawberries or black cherries.

110 g (4 oz) fresh wholemeal
   breadcrumbs
55 g (2 oz) finely chopped hazelnuts
55 g (2 oz) light brown sugar
½ tsp ground cinnamon
250 ml (8 fl oz) double cream

125 ml (4 fl oz) single cream
3 tbsp golden rum
55 g (2 oz) icing sugar
chocolate sauce (recipe page 24) and toasted
   coarsely chopped hazelnuts, to serve

Preheat oven to 200°C (400°F/gas mark 6). In a bowl, mix breadcrumbs, hazelnuts, brown sugar and cinnamon. Spread out evenly on a baking tray. Bake for about 10 minutes, turning mixture over occasionally, until sugar has caramelised, crumbs are crisp and hazelnuts are toasted. Allow to cool completely, then break up into small pieces with a rolling pin. Set aside.

Whisk creams together with rum in a bowl until they hold their shape. Sieve over icing sugar and fold in with a metal spoon. Transfer mixture to a freezer container and freeze for 2–3 hours or until slushy. Remove from freezer, tip into a bowl and whisk to break up any ice crystals. Stir in crumb mixture and return to freezer container. Cover and freeze for several hours or overnight until firm. About 20 minutes before serving, transfer ice cream to fridge so it has time to soften. Serve ice cream in scoops topped with chocolate sauce and a scattering of toasted chopped hazelnuts.

Serves 4

espresso & almond praline semifreddo

see variations page 198

Not a mousse nor an ice cream, this semifrozen Italian dessert falls somewhere in between. Made with cream and eggs, semifreddo translates as "half cold." This needs to be eaten quickly after serving, before it melts.

55 g (2 oz) blanched almonds
140 g (5 oz) light brown sugar
2 tbsp instant espresso coffee granules
100 ml (3½ fl oz) hot water
2 tbsp amaretto liqueur

55 g (2 oz) light brown sugar
3 large egg yolks
250 ml (8 fl oz) double cream
2 tbsp toasted chopped almonds

Grease a baking tray or line it with baking parchment. Put almonds and 4 tablespoons sugar in a small heavy pan and heat gently until sugar melts, stirring occasionally. Cook until sugar caramelises and turns golden brown, then immediately tip almonds and caramel onto prepared baking tray and leave until cold and hard. Grind almond praline to a coarse powder in food processor. Line bases of six 100-g (4-ounce) moulds or cups with waxed paper. Stir coffee into hot water until it dissolves. Cool slightly before stirring in liqueur. Allow to cool completely. In a large bowl, whisk together egg yolks and remaining sugar until pale and creamy. Gradually whisk in cold coffee. Whip cream until just holding its shape and fold in with almond praline until evenly combined. Spoon mixture into moulds, cover with foil and freeze for 8 hours or overnight. To serve, turn out onto dessert plates and peel off lining paper. Sprinkle with chopped almonds and serve immediately.

Serves 6

vanilla ice cream with black cherry compote

see variations page 199

For flavouring ice cream, a vanilla pod is much better than vanilla essence, as essences tend to deteriorate during the freezing process and lose their flavour.

for the ice cream
250 ml (8 fl oz) single cream
1 vanilla pod
4 large egg yolks
110 g (4 oz) caster sugar

250 ml (8 fl oz) double cream
for the black cherry compote
450 g (1 lb) fresh black cherries, stoned
200 g (7 oz) caster sugar

To make ice cream, pour single cream into a heavy saucepan. Split vanilla pod lengthwise and scrape seeds into pan. In a bowl, mix egg yolks and sugar together. Heat cream until it comes to the boil and then slowly pour it into egg mixture, stirring constantly with a wooden spoon. Return mixture to pan and stir over low heat until it coats the back of the spoon. Do not let it boil. Pour into a bowl and set aside until completely cool, stirring occasionally. Beat double cream until thick, then fold into custard mixture. Pour mixture into a freezer container and freeze until partially frozen. Scrape out mixture into a chilled bowl and whisk until smooth. Return to freezer, cover and freeze until solid. To make compote, heat cherries gently in a saucepan sprinkled with sugar until juice runs from cherries and sugar dissolves. Transfer ice cream from freezer to fridge about 30 minutes before serving to give it time to soften. Serve with warm or cold cherry compote spooned on top.

Serves 6

limoncello ice cream

see variations page 200

Adding liqueur to ice cream gives it a softer texture and avoids the necessity of beating the freezing mixture two or three times to break up ice crystals (the alcohol in the liqueur acts like antifreeze in a car).

3 large lemons
85 g (3 oz) icing sugar

275 ml (9 fl oz) double cream
100 ml (3½ fl oz) limoncello

Using a vegetable peeler, shave rind from lemons in long strips. Squeeze lemon juice into a bowl and stir in sugar until dissolved. Add strips of rind and set aside in a cool place to macerate for 30 minutes or longer. Remove rind and discard. Add cream and limoncello to bowl and whip until mixture just holds its shape.

Transfer to a freezer container, coverand freeze for several hours or overnight until solid. Transfer container to fridge about 15 minutes before serving to make it easier to form into scoops.

Serves 6

peach melba yogurt ice

see variations page 201

Both the creamy peach ice and raspberry water ice make great family desserts.

for the peach ice
6 medium-sized fresh peaches
juice of 1 lemon
3 large egg yolks
150 g (5½ oz) caster sugar
125 ml (4 fl oz) milk
150 ml (5½ fl oz) natural Greek yogurt
for the raspberry ice
450 g (1 lb) fresh raspberries

150 g (5½ oz) caster sugar
200 ml (7 fl oz) water
juice of 1 lemon
juice of 1 orange
2 large egg whites
to serve
extra raspberries and small peach slices
raspberry coulis (page 24)

To make peach ice, put peaches in a bowl, cover with boiling water, leave for 1 minute and drain. Peel and stone. Purée peach flesh with lemon juice. Whisk together yolks and sugar until creamy. Heat milk gently until it comes to the boil, then whisk into yolk mixture. Pour back into pan and stir over low heat until custard thickens. Remove from heat and allow to cool. Fold peach purée and yogurt into custard, pour into freezer container and cover. To make raspberry ice, sprinkle raspberries with 2 tablespoons sugar, then stand for 30 minutes. Blend, strain and discard seeds. Heat remaining sugar and water, bring to the boil and simmer 5 minutes. Remove from heat and stir in raspberry purée, lemon and orange juices. Pour into freezer container and cover. Freeze both ices until firm around edges. Whisk, return to freezer for 1 hour, then whisk again. Whisk egg whites until stiff and gradually mix with partially frozen raspberry mixture. Return to freezer for 1 hour, then whisk again. Fill freezer container with alternate scoops of each ice. Swirl together and freeze. Transfer to refrigerator 30 minutes before serving in scoops topped with raspberries, peach slices and raspberry coulis.

Serves 8–10

pomegranate & lychee granita

see variations page 202

A granita is similar to a sorbet, but while a sorbet has a smooth, silky texture, a granita is rougher and formed of large ice crystals made by breaking up the frozen mixture with a fork. Two contrasting coloured granitas made with different fruits make a pretty and eye-catching dessert when layered in glasses.

for the pomegranate granita
350 ml (12 fl oz) pomegranate juice drink
85 g (3 oz) granulated sugar
for the lychee granita
225 g (8 oz) fresh lychees

85 g (3 oz) granulated sugar
250 ml (8 fl oz) water
to decorate
pomegranate seeds and peeled lychees

To make pomegranate granita, heat pomegranate juice and sugar gently until sugar dissolves. Set aside until cold, then pour into a freezer container. To make lychee granita, peel lychees and remove stones. In a food processor or liquidiser, purée with sugar. Add water and blend briefly until mixed in. Strain purée into a freezer container.

Freeze both containers of granitas for about 2 hours or until partially frozen. Beat with a fork to mash unfrozen and frozen parts together until slushy. Return granitas to freezer for 1 hour, then break up with a fork again. Cover and return to freezer until needed. Transfer containers from freezer to fridge about 30 minutes before serving. Break up with a fork again to give a coarse texture and layer in dessert glasses. Serve topped with a few pomegranate seeds and peeled lychees.

Serves 8

blackcurrant sorbet

see variations page 203

In Victorian times, a 'sorbet' always contained alcohol, arriving on the smartest dinner tables in the guise of frozen rum punches or claret cups. In the twentieth century a sorbet has come to mean a low-cal fruit ice, similar to a 'sherbet', but with no dairy products added.

100 g (3½ oz) granulated sugar
200 ml (7 fl oz) water
1 tbsp glucose syrup
500 g (18 oz) fresh blackcurrants

juice of 1 lemon
2 tbsp crème de cassis
1 large egg white

Place sugar, water and syrup in a pan and heat gently until sugar dissolves, stirring occasionally. Simmer for 5 minutes, then set aside to cool.

Strip blackcurrants from their stalks and simmer in a pan with lemon juice until the currants 'pop'. Por into a food processor or liquidiser, add crème de cassis and blend until smooth. Stir, pour into a freezer container and freeze until firm around the edges. Transfer to a bowl and whisk to break up crystals. In another bowl, whisk egg white until standing in soft peaks, then whisk into blackcurrant mixture, 1 tablespoon at a time.

Return sorbet to freezer container, cover and freeze again until solid. About 30 minutes before serving, transfer container to fridge to soften enough to be served in scoops.

Serves 8

red fruits slushy

see variations page 204

A food processor or liquidiser with a powerful motor is needed to crush ice, so if you're unsure whether your machine is strong enough, break up the ice cubes first by placing them in a plastic bag and hitting them with a rolling pin or hammer. If you can't get fresh summer fruits, buy a package of mixed frozen berries and currants and blend them with the fruit juices while they are still solid, omitting the ice cubes.

500 g (18 oz) mixed summer fruits (e.g.,
    strawberries, raspberries, blackcurrants, red
    currants, blueberries, blackberries)
20 ice cubes

125 ml (4 fl oz) apple juice
125 ml (4 fl oz) orange juice
extra fruit, to serve

Prepare fruit as necessary by removing stalks and hulls. Put half the ice cubes in a food processor or liquidiser, add fruit and fruit juices and blend until ice is broken up. Add remaining ice cubes and blend again until mixture is slushy.

Spoon into glasses or serving dishes, top with extra fruit and serve immediately before the ice has time to melt.

Serves 6

orange & cranberry ice lollies

see variations page 205

These vividly coloured ice lollies not only look good, they taste good as well and will appeal to both kids and grown ups alike. As fruit juice freezes, it expands, so don't fill the moulds quite to the top.

3 large oranges   **250 ml (8 fl oz) cranberry juice**

Peel oranges and divide into segments, removing all the pith and pips. In a food processor or liquidiser, blend orange flesh until smooth. Pour into a measuring jug – you will need 250 ml (8 fl oz) to make the ice lollies. If you don't have sufficient, top up by blending an extra orange or with fresh orange juice.

Pour blended orange into 8 ice lolly moulds until they are half full. Freeze until juice is almost solid, but still just soft enough for the sticks to be pushed in and solid enough to hold the sticks in place.

Push in popsicle sticks and top off with cranberry juice. Do not fill all the way to the top. Return to freezer for several hours until frozen solid before carefully removing ice lollies from moulds.

Serves 8 (using 75-ml (3-fl oz) moulds)

variations

strawberry semifreddo

see base recipe page 173

apricot semifreddo
Prepare the basic recipe, replacing the strawberries with the same quantity of tinned apricot halves (drained weight). Purée the apricots in a food processor, rather than crushing them, the purée for the sauce doesn't need to be sieved.

strawberry & orange semifreddo
Prepare the basic recipe, whisking the finely grated zest of 1 orange with the cream and replacing the lemon juice with orange juice.

strawberry & liqueur semifreddo
Prepare the basic recipe, folding in 2 tablespoons brandy or amaretto liqueur with the cream.

strawberry & almond semifreddo
Prepare the basic recipe. Finely chop 85 grams (3 ounces) toasted almonds or hazelnuts and, with a palette knife, press them over the top and sides of the semifreddo.

fruits-of-the-forest semifreddo
Prepare the basic recipe, replacing ¾ of the strawberries with a mix of other berries such as raspberries, blueberries and blackcurrants. The mixed fruit can either be crushed with a potato masher or blended in a food processor.

coconut malibu alaska

see base recipe page 174

raspberry & strawberry alaska
Prepare basic recipe, replacing the mango with 225 grams (8 ounces) raspberries, the coconut liqueur with framboise liqueur and vanilla ice cream with strawberry ice cream.

coconut, mango & chocolate alaska
Prepare basic recipe, replacing the vanilla ice cream with chocolate ice cream and the gingerbread with a dark chocolate cake.

rhubarb & orange alaska
Prepare basic recipe, replacing the mango with rhubarb. Chop 450 grams (1 pound) rhubarb stalks into 2.5-cm (1-inch) lengths and cook in a pan with 85 grams (3 ounces) caster sugar and grated rind and juice of 1 orange until soft. Cool completely before spooning into centre of ice cream. Omit coconut liqueur.

toffee & peach alaska
Prepare basic recipe, replacing mango with 2 peeled, puréed peaches and omitting coconut liqueur. Replace vanilla ice cream with toffee ice cream and serve with toffee sauce.

coffee & apricot alaska
Prepare basic recipe, replacing mango with 5–6 puréed apricots and omitting coconut liqueur. Use coffee ice cream instead of vanilla.

blackberry & mint parfait with amaretti

see base recipe page 176

strawberry parfait with amaretti
Prepare basic recipe, replacing blackberries with strawberries and omitting mint. Serve with strawberry dessert sauce.

blueberry parfait with ginger crumbs
Prepare basic recipe, replacing blackberries with blueberries and replacing amaretti with crushed gingernaps. Serve with raspberry dessert sauce.

mango & lime parfait with amaretti
Prepare basic recipe, replacing blackberries with the same quantity of prepared mango flesh. Omit mint and use lime juice instead of lemon. Serve with strawberry dessert sauce. As mangoes are sweeter than blackberries, reduce the sugar by half or to taste.

peach & rosemary parfait with amaretti
Prepare basic recipe, replacing blackberries with chopped peaches. Replace mint with very finely chopped fresh rosemary. Serve with fresh orange slices.

fruits-of-the-forest parfait with amaretti
Prepare basic recipe, replacing blackberries with mixed berries and currants.

variations

brown bread & hazelnut ice cream

see base recipe page 178

brown bread & raisin ice cream
Prepare basic recipe, adding 85 grams (3 ounces) raisins with bread crumb mixture.

festive Christmas ice cream
Prepare basic recipe, adding 25 grams (1 ounce) each dried cranberries and sultanas, 5 tablespoons chopped dried apricots and 1 tablespoon finely chopped crystallised orange peel with the bread crumb mixture.

brown bread, brandy & prune ice cream
Prepare basic recipe, soaking 175 grams (6 ounces) stoned, finely chopped prunes in 3 tablespoons brandy for 1 hour. Stir in prunes and their juice with the breadcrumb mixture.

atholl brose ice cream
Prepare basic recipe, replacing breadcrumbs with rolled oats. Omit icing sugar and whip creams with 2 tablespoons whisky, instead of rum and 4 tablespoons honey.

amaretti & hazelnut ice cream
Prepare basic recipe, omitting light brown sugar. Replace breadcrumbs with crushed amaretti biscuits, mixed with hazelnuts and cinnamon without baking in oven. Replace rum with amaretto liqueur.

variations

espresso & almond praline semifreddo

see base recipe page 180

espresso & chocolate honeycomb semifreddo
Prepare basic recipe, replacing almond praline with 100 grams (3½ ounces) chocolate honeycomb sweets (such as Crunchie bar) chopped very finely.

espresso & hazelnut praline semifreddo
Prepare basic recipe, replacing almonds in praline with whole hazelnuts and the amaretto with coffee liqueur. Serve with toasted chopped hazelnuts instead of almonds.

espresso & chocolate chip semifreddo
Prepare basic recipe, omitting almond praline. Fold 100 grams (3½ ounces) plain chocolate chips in with whipped cream. Replace amaretto with brandy.

espresso, almond praline & orange semifreddo
Prepare basic recipe, replacing liqueur with orange juice. Whip grated rind of 1 orange with the cream.

espresso & amaretti semifreddo
Prepare basic recipe, replacing almond praline with 110 grams (4 ounces) crushed amaretti and 85 grams (3 ounces) chopped toasted pecans. Scatter extra pecans over finished dessert.

vanilla ice cream with black cherry compote

see base recipe page 183

vanilla & chocolate chip ice cream with black cherry compote
Prepare basic recipe, adding 100 grams (3½ ounces) plain chocolate chips when whisking partially frozen custard.

vanilla & lemon ripple ice cream with black cherry compote
Prepare basic recipe, whisking partially frozen custard and then folding in 4 tablespoons lemon curd (page 109) before returning to freezer.

vanilla & peanut cookie ice cream with black cherry compote
Prepare basic recipe, whisking partially frozen custard, and then folding in 6 peanut butter biscuits, crushed, before returning to freezer.

vanilla ice cream with strawberry compote
Prepare basic recipe, replacing cherry compote with strawberry compote. Place 450 grams (1 pound) fresh strawberries in a bowl, sprinkle with 3 tablespoons icing sugar and 2 tablespoons orange juice, and let stand for 30 minutes before serving.

vanilla & prune ice cream with black cherry compote
Prepare basic recipe, freezing custard until partially frozen. Soak 6 stoned, chopped prunes in 4 tablespoons green tea for 30 minutes. After whisking semifrozen custard until smooth, fold in prunes and any tea remaining in bowl before returning to freezer.

variations

limoncello ice cream

see base recipe page 184

orange liqueur ice cream
Prepare basic recipe, replacing lemons with 2 oranges. Replace limoncello with an orange liqueur such as Cointreau and Grand Marnier.

mojito ice cream
Prepare basic recipe, replacing lemons with 6 limes and 2 teaspoons chopped fresh mint. Replace limoncello with white rum.

harvey wallbanger ice cream
Prepare basic recipe, replacing lemons with 2 oranges and the limoncello with 4 tablespoons vodka and 2 tablespoons Galliano.

piña colada ice cream
Prepare basic recipe, replacing lemons with 100 ml (3½ fl oz) pineapple juice and the limoncello with coconut liqueur.

margarita ice cream
Prepare basic recipe, replacing lemons with 6 limes and the limoncello with 4 tablespoons tequila and 4 tablespoons orange liqueur.

peach melba yogurt ice

see base recipe page 185

pineapple raspberry yogurt ice
Prepare basic recipe, replacing peaches with roughly chopped flesh of
1 ripe pineapple.

mango raspberry yogurt ice
Prepare basic recipe, replacing peaches with flesh of 3 ripe mangoes, puréed
with juice of 2 limes rather than lemon juice.

nectarine blueberry yogurt ice
Prepare basic recipe, replacing peaches with nectarines and the raspberries
with blueberries.

apricot raspberry yogurt ice
Prepare basic recipe, replacing peaches with 12 apricots, halved and stoned.

apple blackberry yogurt ice
Prepare basic recipe, replacing peaches with roughly chopped apples, cooked
in a covered pan with lemon juice until soft enough to purée. Replace
raspberries with blackberries.

pomegranate & lychee granita

see base recipe page 187

rhubarb granita

Prepare basic lychee granita recipe, replacing lychees with 450 grams
(1 pound) rhubarb stalks cut into 2.5-cm (1-inch) lengths. Simmer rhubarb
with water and sugar, increasing sugar by 175 grams (6 ounces) and adding
grated rind of 1 orange. When soft, purée and freeze as for lychee granita.
Omit pomegranate granita.

pink grapefruit granita

Prepare basic pomegranate granita recipe, replacing pomegranate juice with
pink grapefruit juice and add 2 extra tablespoons sugar. Omit lychee granita.

apple-orange granita

Prepare basic recipe for pomegranate granita. Replace half the pomegranate
juice with apple juice and half with orange juice. Omit lychee granita.

mango granita

Prepare basic recipe for lychee granita, replacing lychees with the same
quantity of prepared mango flesh. Omit pomegranate granita.

papaya-litreime granita

Prepare basic recipe for lychee granita, replacing lychees with the same
quantity of prepared papaya flesh and adding grated rind and juice of
2 limes. Omit pomegranate granita.

variations

blackcurrant sorbet

see base recipe page 189

raspberry sorbet
Prepare basic recipe, replacing blackcurrants with raspberries and crème de cassis with framboise liqueur. Strain puréed raspberries to remove seeds.

chocolate sorbet
Prepare basic recipe, omitting blackcurrants, lemon juice and crème de cassis. Increase the sugar to 175 grams (6 ounces) and the water to 500 ml (15 fl oz). Put sugar, water and syrup in a pan and whisk in 55 grams (2 ounces) cocoa powder. Bring to the boil and simmer for 5 minutes. Remove from heat and stir in 55 grams (2 ounces) chopped plain chocolate and 1 teaspoon vanilla essence until chocolate melts. Freeze and then whisk in the egg white.

lemon sorbet
Prepare basic recipe, omitting blackcurrants and crème de cassis. Increase sugar to 450 grams (1 pound) and water to 750 ml (1¼ pints). Dissolve sugar in the water with the syrup and stir in 250 ml (8 fl oz) lemon juice and grated rind of 2 lemons. Simmer for 2–3 minutes. Cool, freeze and whisk in egg white.

blueberry sorbet
Prepare basic recipe, replacing blackcurrants with blueberries.

variations

red fruits slushy

see base recipe page 190

pear, apricot & banana slushy
Prepare basic recipe, replacing fruits with equal weight of chopped pears, apricots and bananas. Replace apple juice with pineapple juice.

papaya, carrot & watermelon slushy
Prepare basic recipe, replacing fruits with equal weight of chopped papaya, watermelon and bananas. Chop fruit into pieces and process with 2 tablespoons dried milk powder and equal quantities apple and carrot juice and ice. Omit orange juice.

mango & pink grapefruit slushy
Prepare basic recipe, replacing fruits with 450 grams (1 pound) mango. Process with orange and pink grapefruit juice and ice in place of apple juice.

melon & lychee slushy
Prepare basic recipe, replacing fruits with 225 grams (8 ounces) cantaloupe and 225 grams (8 ounces) lychee flesh. Blend with 250 ml (8 fl oz) apple juice and ice. Omit orange juice.

nectarine & grape slushy
Prepare basic recipe, replacing fruits with equal weight of chopped nectarines and seedless green and red grapes and omitting juices. Blend with 250 ml (8 fl oz) white or red grape juice and ice.

orange & cranberry ice pops

see base recipe page 193

pineapple & red grape ice pops
Prepare basic recipe, omitting oranges and cranberry juice. Use 250 ml
(8 fl oz) each of pineapple juice and red grape juice.

cherry & kiwi ice pops
Prepare basic recipe, puréeing 110 grams (4 ounces) stoned black or dark red
cherries with 1 teaspoon honey and 125 ml (4 fl oz) fromage frais to replace
orange juice. To replace cranberry juice, purée 110 grams (4 ounces) kiwi
fruit flesh with 1 teaspoon honey and 125 ml (4 fl oz) fromage frais

banana, strawberry & coconut ice pops
Instead of basic recipe, purée 1 small, peeled and chopped banana with
175 grams (6 ounces) hulled strawberries, 175 ml (6 fl oz) milk and 80 ml
(3 fl oz) coconut milk. Pour into moulds and freeze.

mango & yogurt ice pops
Instead of basic recipe, purée flesh of 1 medium-sized ripe mango with the
single cream and 150 ml (5 fl oz) natural yogurt. Pour into moulds and
freeze.

pomegranate & grapefruit ice pops
Instead of basic recipe, use 250 ml (8 fl oz) each of pomegranate juice and
grapefruit juice.

biscuits,
brownies,
shortcakes &
whoopie pies

Small enough to satisfy young appetites, grown-up

enough for adults to savour – no one will be able

to resist caramel and pecan turtle brownies,

vanilla whoopie pies, peanut butter biscuits and ice

cream sandwiches and all the other treats on the

following pages.

rocky road biscuits

see variations page 223

These will be a guaranteed hit with children and adults alike. They can be served on their own or with scoops of your favourite ice cream.

100 g (4 oz) plain chocolate, chopped
1 tbsp golden syrup
110 g (4 oz) unsalted butter, cut into
    small pieces
55 g (2 oz) cream cheese
12 digestive biscuits, in small pieces

85 g (3 oz) dried apricots, chopped
25 g (1 oz) dried cranberries
55 g (2 oz) chopped pecans
110 g (4 oz) mini marshmallows
55 g milk chocolate, melted

Put dark chocolate, golden syrup and butter in a large saucepan (one that will be big enough to hold all the ingredients). Heat gently until melted, stirring from time to time until smooth. Remove from heat and stir in cream cheese until evenly combined. Add broken biscuits, dried apricots, cranberries, pecans and about three-quarters of the marshmallows. Stir well until all ingredients are well coated.

Line cups of a 12-cup muffin tin with clingfilm. Spoon in mixture, pressing it down with the back of the spoon. Top with remaining marshmallows and set in the fridge.

Lift biscuits carefully out of the cups and peel off clingfilm. Drizzle melted milk chocolate over the top of biscuits. Let set again.

Makes 12

lemon & poppy seed shortbread fingers with plums & cherries

see variations page 224

The secret of good shortbread is to work in a cool kitchen and handle the dough as lightly as you possibly can. Too much kneading or processing and the end result will be heavy and solid rather than buttery, melt-in-the-mouthand crisp.

for the shortbread
175 g (6 oz) unsalted butter, softened
85 g (3 oz) granulated sugar, plus extra
    to dust
finely grated rind of 1 lemon
2 tbsp poppy seeds
175 g (6 oz) plain flour
85 g (3 oz) rice flour

for the fruit
8 red plums, halved and stoned
225 g (8 oz) red cherries, stoned
200 ml (7 oz) apple juice
1 red fruit tea bag (e.g. raspberry, cherry,
    strawberry)

Preheat oven to 150°C (300°F/gas mark 2). Grease a shallow 18x28-cm (7x11-inch) tin and line base with parchment. To make the shortbread, beat butter, sugar and lemon rind together until light and creamy. Add poppy seeds, sieve in the flours and work mixture together lightly by hand (or in a food processor). Transfer to tin and with floured hands, press mixture to fill pan evenly. Prick surface all over with a fork and bake for 45 minutes until pale golden brown. Dust top with sugar and mark cut lines for squares or triangles. Cool in tin for 15 minutes, then lift shortbread onto a wire rack to cool completely. Remove lining paper and cut into pieces. To cook the plums and cherries, place in a pan with apple juice tucking tea bag under fruit. Bring to the boil, then remove from heat. Cover pan and allow fruit to cool in the liquid. Remove tea bag and serve fruit with shortbread.
Makes 6

caramel & pecan turtle brownies

see variations page 225

Decadently rich and dark with a golden toffee and nut topping, these "millionaire" brownies are the ultimate feel-good dessert.

for the brownies
100 g (3½ oz) plain chocolate, chopped
175 g (6 oz) unsalted butter, cut up
3 large eggs, beaten
150 g (5½ oz) dark brown sugar
55 g (2 oz) plain flour
1 tsp baking powder
55 g (2 oz) roughly chopped pecans
55 g (2 oz) white chocolate chips

for the topping
175 g (6 oz) granulated sugar
2 tbsp cold water
175 ml (6 fl oz) double cream
1 tsp vanilla essence
125 g (5 oz) unsalted butter
110 g (4 oz) roughly chopped pecans
110 g (4 oz) plain or milk chocolate chunks

Preheat oven to 180°C (350°F). Grease a 20-cm (8-inch) loose-bottomed square cake tin and line the base and sides with parchment. Melt plain chocolate and butter in a pan over a gentle heat until melted, stirring occasionally until smooth. Allow to cool for 10 minutes. Beat in eggs, brown sugar, flour, baking powder, pecans and white chocolate chips until evenly combined. Pour into pan and bake for 30 minutes until crusty on top but still soft underneath. Allow to cool in tin. To make the topping, heat sugar and water, bring to the boil and bubble until syrup caramelises to a dark brown. Remove from heat and gradually beat in cream. (If caramel sets in hard lumps, microwave mixture on medium power to re-melt, stirring every 30 seconds.) Add vanilla. In a separate bowl, beat butter until creamy. Gradually beat in caramel mixture. Allow to cool completely and then chill until spreadable. Spread topping over brownies, scatter pecans and chocolate chunks on top and allow to set before removing from pan and cutting into squares.
Makes 9

chocolate brownie gâteau

see variations page 226

The perfect dessert that can also double as a birthday cake for anyone who finds chocolate brownies irresistible – and, let's face it, that means most of us! Keep an eye on the brownie layers towards the end of the cooking time. If they're left too long in the oven, the centres will dry out rather than remaining gooey and dark.

200 g (9 oz) unsalted butter, softened
200 g (9 oz) plain chocolate, chopped
4 large eggs
200 g (9 oz) light brown sugar
½ tsp vanilla essence

175 g (6 oz) plain flour
200 g (7 oz) whole hazelnuts, chopped
for the filling
125 ml (4 fl oz) crème fraîche
100 g (3½ oz) white chocolate, chopped

Preheat oven to 180°C (350°F/gas mark 4). Grease, then line bases of two 20-cm (8-inch) cake tins with baking parchment. In a saucepan, heat butter and chocolate gently until melted, stirring until smooth. Set aside to cool for 10 minutes. Beat together eggs, sugar and vanilla and add to chocolate mixture with flour and hazelnuts. Stir until evenly combined. Divide mixture between cake tins. Bake for 25–30 minutes or until the tops have a pale crust but the middle is still quite soft. Place a sheet of waxed paper on a cooling rack. Loosen edges of brownie layers with a knife and turn upside down onto rack, still in the tins. Allow to cool before removing tins and lining paper. To make the filling, heat crème fraîche and white chocolate gently until chocolate melts. Stir until smooth, transfer to a bowl and allow to cool and thicken until it holds its shape. Whisk cooled filling until light and creamy and use to sandwich brownie layers together.

Serves 12

vanilla whoopie pies

see variations page 227

These biscuit-litreike cakes filled with marshmallow icing are an all-American favourite adored by kids and adults alike. Perfect for lunch boxes and parties alike.

1 large egg
150 g (5½ oz) granulated sugar
85 g (3 oz) unsalted butter, melted and cooled
275 g (10 oz) plain flour
¾ tsp bicarbonate of soda
200 ml (7 oz) buttermilk
1 tsp vanilla essence

for the filling
2 large egg whites
110 g (4 oz) granulated sugar
½ tsp cream of tartar
110 g (4 oz) white or pink marshmallows
for the topping
175 g (6 oz) icing sugar
about 2 tbsp lemon juice
sugar sprinkles

Preheat oven to 180°C (350°F/gas mark 4). Line 2 baking trays with parchment. In a mixing bowl, whisk egg and sugar until pale and creamy. Drizzle melted butter around edge of mixture and fold in. Sieve in half the flour with the bicarbonate of soda and fold in with half the buttermilk. Sieve in remaining flour, add remaining buttermilk and the vanilla and fold together. Drop 24 small spoonfuls of the mixture well spaced on the baking trays and bake for about 15 minutes until springy. Cool for 10 minutes before removing from baking tray to a wire rack. To make filling, whisk egg whites, sugar and cream of tartar together in a bowl set over a pan of simmering water for about 5 minutes until thickened. Add marshmallows and stir to melt, then whisk for another 2 minutes until shiny and smooth. Allow to cool. Use to sandwich whoopie pies together in pairs. To make topping, sieve icing sugar into a bowl and stir in enough lemon juice to make a spreadable icing. Spread a little over the top of each whoopie pie and scatter on sugar sprinkles. Store in an airtight container.
Makes 12

giant chocolate & orange whoopie pie

see variations page 228

For this party-size pie, a white chocolate filling replaces traditional marshmallow.

275 g (10 oz) plain flour
55 g (2 oz) unsweetened cocoa powder
1 tsp baking powder
½ tsp bicarbonate of soda
110 g (4 oz) unsalted butter
85 g (3 oz) dark brown sugar
150 g (5 oz) granulated sugar
finely grated rind of 1 orange
2 large eggs
125 ml (4 fl oz) soured cream
2 tbsp milk

for the filling
110 g (4 oz) full-fat cream cheese
40 g (1½ oz) caster sugar
100 g (3½ oz) white chocolate, melted
60 ml (2 fl oz) double cream, whipped
for the icing
225 g (8 oz) icing sugar, sieved
about 3 tbsp orange juice
few drops of orange food colouring
grated chocolate or chocolate curls

Preheat oven to 180°C (350°F/gas mark 4). Draw two 18-cm (7-inch) circles on two sheets of baking parchment, place on baking trays. Sieve together flour, cocoa, baking powder and bicarbonate of soda. In a bowl, beat butter, sugars and orange rind together until creamy. Gradually beat in eggs, then stir in dry ingredients alternating with soured cream and milk. Spoon mixture onto baking trays and spread to fill circles. Bake for 20 minutes until firm. Cool for 10 minutes, then transfer to wire rack. To make filling, beat cream cheese and sugar until smooth. Add melted chocolate and fold in with cream. Use to sandwich cake layers together. To make icing, mix icing sugar with enough orange juice to make smooth icing. Tint with orange food colouring and spoon over cake. Scatter with grated chocolate or curls.
Serves 10

strawberries & cream scones

see variations page 229

Make sure you leave plenty of room at the end of the meal for one – or more - of these indulgent treats, as they're impossible to resist. Make the scones ahead and assemble with the cream and strawberries about 30 minutes before serving.

for the scones
110 g (4 oz) unsalted butter, cut into
    small pieces
385 g (13 oz) self-raising flour
110g (4 oz) granulated sugar
80 ml (3 fl oz) warm milk, plus a little extra
    milk for glazing

1 large egg, beaten
½ tsp vanilla essence
1 tbsp lemon juice
for the filling
275 ml (9 fl oz) whipping or double cream
3 tbsp strawberry jam
275 g (10 oz) fresh strawberries

Put butter and flour in mixing bowl and rub together until consistency of breadcrumbs. Stir in sugar, warm milk, beaten egg, vanilla and lemon juice. Mix to make a soft, smooth dough. Preheat oven to 220°C (425°F/gas mark 7). On a lightly floured surface, roll out dough about 2 cm (¾ inch) thick. Cut out 8 rounds using a 6-cm (2½-inch) plain or fluted pastry cutter, gathering up trimmings of dough and rerolling as needed. Lift dough rounds onto a greased baking tray and brush tops with milk to glaze. Bake for 10-12 minutes or until well risen and golden brown. Scones are cooked when they sound hollow if tapped on the base. Transfer to a wire rack to cool. Whip cream until it holds its shape. Split each scone in half and spread the bottom halves with jam. Spoon on cream, then add sliced strawberries and top halves of the scones.

Makes 8

peanut butter biscuit & ice cream sandwiches

see variations page 230

The biscuits can be made several days ahead and stored in an airtight container. Any ice cream can be used to sandwich the biscuits together, so just pick your family's favourite.

for the biscuits
125 g (4½ oz) unsalted butter, softened
½ tsp vanilla essence
finely grated rind of ½ lemon
85 g (3 oz) caster sugar
25 g (1 oz) light brown sugar
85 g (3 oz) crunchy peanut butter
175 g (6 oz) plain flour
1 tsp bicarbonate of soda

25 g (1 oz) unsalted peanuts, chopped
for the filling
1 tub of ice cream of your choice, softened
for the chocolate sauce
110 g (4 oz) plain chocolate, chopped
15 g (½ oz) unsalted butter, cut up
3 tbsp milk

To make biscuits, preheat the oven to 180°C (350°F/gas mark 4). Grease 2 or 3 baking trays and line with parchment. Cream together butter, vanilla, lemon rind, sugar, brown sugar and peanut butter. Sieve in flour and bicarbonate of soda and stir in peanuts, working with your hands to make a soft dough. With floured hands, roll dough into 20 small balls and place on baking trays, well spaced apart. Press down lightly on top of each with a fork. Bake for 15–20 minutes until light golden. Allow to cool on trays. For filling, sandwich biscuits together with a scoop of ice cream, pressing the top cookie down gently. Place in freezer and freeze until ice cream is firm. To make the chocolate sauce, gently heat chocolate, butter and milk in a pan until chocolate and butter melt, stirring regularly until smooth. When ready to serve, place ice cream sandwiches on serving plates and drizzle with chocolate sauce.
Makes 10

fruit & nut chocolate slices with crème fraîche

see variations page 231

Macadamia nuts with their buttery, almost shortbread-litreike flavour, turn these simple chocolate slices, which are somewhere between a mousse and a cake, into something special. If you like the current craze for adding salted nuts or salt caramel to chocolate bars, try using salted macadamias, but if not, the plain variety are readily available.

200 g (7 oz) dark chocolate, chopped
150 g (5½ oz) dark brown sugar
175 g (6 oz) unsalted butter, cut up
125 ml (4 fl oz) milk
1 tsp vanilla essence

3 large eggs, beaten
85 g (3 oz) raisins
85 g (3 oz) macadamia nuts, roughly chopped
crème fraîche, grated chocolate and icing sugar, to serve

Preheat oven to 180°C (350°F/gas mark 4). Grease a 20-cm (8-inch) square tin and line base and sides with nonstick baking parchment. Place chocolate in a pan with brown sugar, butter and milk. Heat gently until melted, stirring occasionally until smooth. Remove from heat and allow to cool for 10 minutes. Beat in vanilla essence and eggs until evenly mixed and then stir in raisins and chopped macadamia nuts. Pour mixture into prepared tin and bake for 30–35 minutes or until the top is firm when lightly pressed. Allow to cool in the tin, then transfer to the fridge and chill for 3–4 hours or longer. Remove cake from tin and peel off lining paper. Cut into 8 large or 12 smaller fingers and serve with crème fraîche with with grated chocolate sprinkled over the top and a light dusting of icing sugar.

Serves 8–12

variations

rocky road biscuits

see base recipe page 207

rocky road milk chocolate biscuits
Prepare basic recipe, replacing the plain chocolate with milk chocolate and drizzling with white chocolate instead of milk chocolate.

rocky road biscuits with crunchy seeds
Prepare basic recipe, adding a mixture of seeds such as sunflower, sesame and pumpkin in place of the dried apricots and cranberries.

rocky road meringue biscuits
Prepare basic recipe, replacing marshmallows with 8 small crushed meringues and stirring them into the mixture.

rocky road ginger biscuits
Prepare basic recipe, replacing digestive biscuits with gingersnaps.

rocky road cinnamon biscuits
Prepare basic recipe, adding 1 teaspoon ground cinnamon to the plain chocolate, syrup and butter mixture.

variations

lemon & poppy seed shortbread fingers with plums & cherries

see base recipe page 208

orange & poppy seed shortbread fingers with plums & cherries
Prepare basic shortbread recipe, replacing lemon rind with orange rind.

lemon & sesame seed shortbread fingers with plums & cherries
Prepare basic shortbread recipe, replacing poppy seeds with sesame seeds.

lemon, poppy seed & almond shortbread fingers with plums & cherries
Prepare basic shortbread recipe, replacing rice flour with ground almonds.

**lemon, poppy seed & chocolate shortbread fingers with
plums & cherries**
Prepare basic shortbread recipe, drizzling baked, cooled shortbread fingers
with 85 grams (3 ounces) melted dark chocolate.

lemon & hazelnut wholemeal shortbread fingers with plums & cherries
Prepare basic shortbread recipe, replacing half the plain flour with
wholemeal flour and the poppy seeds with ground hazelnuts.

variations

caramel & pecan turtle brownies

see base recipe page 210

cardamom-spiced turtle brownies
Prepare basic recipe, adding 1 teaspoon ground cardamom to plain chocolate and butter mixture.

caramel & walnut turtle brownies
Prepare basic recipe, replacing pecans with walnuts.

pecan brownies with chocolate fudge icing
Prepare basic recipe, replacing caramel topping with chocolate fudge icing. Heat 55 grams (2 ounces) sweet butter with 3 tablespoons milk and 25 grams (1 ounce) cocoa powder until melted. Sieve in 200 grams (7 ounces) icing sugar, beating well after each addition. Let icing cool and thicken, then beat before spreading over brownies.

caramel, pecan & sultana turtle brownies
Prepare basic recipe, using sultanas instead of white chocolate chips.

vanilla-iced pecan brownies
Prepare basic recipe, replacing caramel topping on brownies with vanilla-flavoured glacé icing. Sieve 200 grams (7 ounces) icing sugar into a bowl and stir in ½ teaspoon vanilla essence and enough cold water to make a smooth icing that can be drizzled over brownies.

variations

chocolate brownie gâteau

see base recipe page 212

chocolate pecan brownie gâteau
Prepare basic recipe, replacing chopped hazelnuts with chopped pecans.

chocolate brownie gâteau with plain chocolate cream
Prepare basic recipe, replacing white chocolate in the filling with
dark chocolate.

chocolate brownie gâteau with raspberries and white chocolate cream
Prepare basic recipe, spreading bottom brownie layer with half the filling
and then scattering over 110 grams (4 ounces) fresh raspberries. Add
remaining filling and top brownie layer.

chocolate raisin brownie gâteau
Prepare basic recipe, replacing chopped hazelnuts with raisins.

chocolate orange brownie gâteau
Prepare basic recipe, adding finely grated rind of 1 orange to brownie batter
and serving the gâteau with fresh orange segments.

vanilla whoopie pies

see base recipe page 215

vanilla whoopie pies with lemon buttercream
Prepare basic recipe, filling whoopie pies with lemon buttercream instead of
marshmallow cream. Beat 110 grams (4 ounces) unsalted butter until softened.
Gradually beat in 225 grams (8 ounces) sieved icing sugar until smooth, adding
the juice of ½ lemon to make a soft spreadable icing.

red, white & blue velvet whoopie pies
Prepare basic recipe, adding 1 tablespoon blue food colouring to the batter and
colouring the topping red.

almond whoopie pies
Prepare basic recipe, replacing vanilla essence in batter with almond essence.
Scatter chopped toasted almonds over the pies rather than sugar sprinkles.

vanilla whoopie pies with cream cheese filling
Prepare basic recipe, replacing marshmallow filling with cream cheese filling.
Beat together 110 grams (4 ounces) full-fat cream cheese, 55 grams (2 ounces)
unsalted butter and 225 grams (8 ounces) sieved icing sugar.

chocolate whoopie pies
Prepare basic recipe, replacing 2 tablespoons of flour in the batter with cocoa.

variations

giant chocolate & orange whoopie pie

see base recipe page 216

giant ginger & orange whoopie pie
Prepare basic recipe, omitting cocoa powder, increasing flour to
350 grams (12 ounces) and adding 1 teaspoon ground ginger with
the other dry ingredients.

giant chocolate & hazelnut whoopie pie
Prepare basic recipe, replacing 55 grams (2 ounces) plain flour with
ground hazelnuts.

giant chocolate & orange whoopie pie with plain chocolate filling
Prepare basic recipe, substituting melted plain chocolate for the white
chocolate in the filling.

giant chocolate & raspberry whoopie pie
Prepare basic recipe, folding 110 grams (4 ounces) lightly crushed raspberries
into filling with the whipped cream. For the icing, replace orange juice and
orange food colouring with cranberry juice or grenadine syrup.

giant lemon, mint & chocolate whoopie pie
Prepare basic recipe, replacing orange rind in batter with grated rind of
2 lemons. Replace orange juice in icing with lemon juice and the orange
food colouring with a few drops of peppermint flavouring.

variations

strawberries & cream scones

see base recipe page 219

melba cream scones
Prepare basic recipe, replacing strawberry jam with seedless raspberry jam and strawberries with 1 peeled and sliced peach and 140 grams (5 ounces) raspberries.

strawberries & cream orange scones
Prepare basic recipe, replacing lemon juice in dough with orange juice and whipping the finely grated rind of 1 orange into cream for filling.

golden raisin scones with cherries & cream
Prepare basic recipe. Add 55 grams (2 ounces) sultanas to dough. Replace strawberries with stoned cherries and strawberry jam with cherry jam.

nutty scones with strawberries & cream
Prepare basic recipe, scattering chopped almonds, pine kernels or pecans over tops of scones after glazing with milk.

cinnamon scones with strawberries & cream
Prepare basic recipe, adding 1 teaspoon ground cinnamon to dough with the flour.

peanut butter biscuit & ice cream sandwiches

see base recipe page 220

cashew butter biscuit & ice cream sandwiches
Prepare basic recipe, replacing peanuts with chopped unsalted cashews and the peanut butter with cashew butter.

peanut butter biscuit & ice cream sandwiches with strawberry sauce
Prepare basic recipe, filling the sandwiches with strawberry ice cream and drizzling with strawberry sauce made by puréeing 110 grams (4 ounces) fresh strawberries with 1 tablespoon icing sugar.

chocolate chip biscuit & ice cream sandwiches
Prepare basic recipe, replacing peanuts with 5 tablespoons milk chocolate chips and the crunchy peanut butter with smooth.

peanut butter raisin cookie & ice cream sandwiches
Prepare basic recipe, replacing peanuts with 55 grams (2 ounces) raisins.

orange peanut cookie and ice cream sandwiches
Prepare basic recipe, replacing lemon rind and vanilla essence in dough with finely grated rind of half an orange.

fruit & nut chocolate slices with crème fraîche

see base recipe page 222

chocolate apricot slices with crème fraîche
Prepare basic recipe, replacing macadamia nuts with chopped dried apricots.

milk chocolate fruit & nut slices with crème fraîche
Prepare basic recipe, replacing plain chocolate with good-quality milk chocolate, the raisins with dried cranberries and the macadamias with chopped unsalted peanuts.

double chocolate & nut slices with crème fraîche
Prepare basic recipe, replacing raisins with 85 grams (3 ounces) white chocolate chips.

chocolate almond slices with crème fraîche
Prepare basic recipe, replacing raisins and macadamia nuts with 55 grams (2 oz) chopped or flaked almonds and 55 grams (2 oz) finely chopped mixed peel or glacé cherries.

fruit & nut chocolate slices with orange crème fraîche
Prepare basic recipe, stirring the finely grated rind of 1 small orange into the crème fraîche.

fritters, crêpes & waffles

Crisp and light fritters, melt-in-the-mouth crêpes
and waffles to die for – this chapter will satisfy all
your comfort food cravings.

fruit tempura

see variations page 248

Unlike most batters, light tempura batter needs to be used as soon as it is made rather than left to stand. It's also important to use chilled water straight from the fridge – sparkling mineral water works best – and not to fry too many pieces of fruit at one time or the temperature of the oil will drop and the batter will be soggy rather than crisp.

1 kg (2 lbs) fresh, ripe, but firm fruit such as
    peaches, apricots, bananas, plums, cherries,
    pineapple
for the orange cream
200 ml (7 fl oz) double cream
finely grated rind and juice of 1 orange

for the batter
85 g (3 oz) plain flour, plus extra for dusting
1 tbsp cornflour
1 tsp baking powder
2 tsp caster sugar
200 g (7 fl oz) well-chilled sparkling mineral
    water
vegetable or peanut oil for deep-frying

Prepare the fruit by peeling and pitting as necessary. Cut into two-bite-size slices, wedges or chunks or leave whole if small. To make the orange cream, whip cream, half the orange rind and the juice together until holding its shape. Spoon into a serving dish, sprinkle with remaining rind and chill, covered with clingfilm, until needed. To make the batter, sieve flour, cornflour and baking powder into a bowl. Stir in sugar. Whisk in water until just combined. Don't overmix the batter – it doesn't matter if it is still a little bit lumpy. Heat oil for deep-frying to 190°C (375°F). Dust fruit with flour, dip in batter and fry 3–4 pieces at a time for 2–3 minutes or until pale golden and crisp. Drain on a plate lined with kitchen paper. Serve immediately with orange cream.

Serves 4

blueberry fritters with apricot sauce

see variations page 249

When fresh apricots are unavailable, the sauce can be made with tinned fruit. Simply blend the contents of one 400 gram (14-ounce) tin of apricot halves in fruit juice with one tablespoon honey until smooth, then warm in a saucepan when needed.

for the sauce
300 g (11 oz) fresh apricots, halved and stoned
200 ml (7 fl oz) apple juice
1 tbsp honey
for the fritters
150 g (5½ oz) fresh blueberries

110 g (4 oz) fresh raspberries
85 g (3 oz) plain flour
2 tbsp milk
1 large egg
2 tbsp caster sugar
vegetable or peanut oil for deep-frying

To make the sauce, simmer apricot halves in a pan with apple juice and honey for about 10 minutes until softened. Pour into liquidiser and blend until smooth. Return to the pan and set aside while you make fritters. To make the fritters, in a bowl, mix together blueberries, raspberries and flour. In another bowl, whisk together milk, egg and sugar and stir into fruit mixture to make a thick batter. Mix well so all the ingredients are combined. Meanwhile, heat oil for deep-frying to 180°C (350°F). Drop spoonfuls of batter into hot oil and fry for 1–2 minutes, turning over once or twice until golden. Drain on a plate lined with kitchen paper and keep warm in a low oven while you continue frying, to make 12 fritters. Reheat sauce over low heat. Divide warm fritters between 4 serving plates and spoon the sauce alongside. Serve immediately.

Serves 4

chinese toffee pineapple & bananas

see variations page 250

A classic Chinese dessert that is a mainstay of Cantonese restaurant menus. The soft sweet fruit encased in crunchy caramel and sesame seeds is a real delight.

110 g (4 oz) plain flour, plus extra
    for dusting
about 125 ml (4 fl oz) cold water
2 tsp vegetable or peanut oil, plus extra for
    deep-frying
3 pineapple rings, canned or fresh

2 large, ripe but firm, bananas
sesame oil for greasing
ice cubes
350 g (12 oz) granulated sugar
175 ml (6 fl oz) water
3 tbsp sesame seeds

Sieve flour into a bowl and whisk in enough cold water to make a smooth batter. Stir in oil. Let stand for 30 minutes. Cut each pineapple ring into quarters. Peel bananas and cut each into 6 equal chunks. Heat oil for deep-frying to 190°C (375°F). Dust fruit with flour and drop about 6 pieces into the batter. Lift them out one at a time with a slotted spoon and carefully lower into hot oil. Adding fruit pieces one at a time keeps them from sticking together as they fry. Fry fruit for 2–3 minutes until golden, then remove with slotted spoon and drain on plate lined with kitchen paper. Repeat with remaining fruit. Grease a large plate with a little sesame oil and have ready a bowl filled with cold water and ice cubes. To make toffee coating, gently heat sugar in a heavy pan with the water, bring to the boil and boil until syrup caramelises to golden brown. Remove pan from heat and add sesame seeds and fruit pieces, turning them over until they are well coated. Immediately turn out onto the greased plate and use 2 forks to dip fruit into the iced water to set toffee coating. Serve immediately. *Serves 4*

thai coconut pancakes with watermelon, star fruit & pomegranate seeds

see variations page 251

As the fried coconut balls cool, they will absorb the hot syrup and become temptingly sweet and sticky. They are best eaten still slightly warm rather than chilled.

for the coconut balls
110 g (4 oz) plain flour
½ tsp baking powder
6 tbsp coconut milk powder
55 g (2 oz) unsalted butter, cut into small
    pieces
about 4 tbsp coconut milk or cow's milk
vegetable or peanut oil for deep-frying

for the syrup
225 g (8 oz) granulated sugar
4 tbsp water
1 tsp coconut flavouring
to serve:
1 slice watermelon
2 pineapple rings
seeds from 1 pomegranate
2 tbsp grated fresh coconut

To make the coconut balls, sieve flour, baking powder and coconut milk powder into a bowl. Rub in butter until consistency of breadcrumbs, then add enough milk to mix to a smooth, soft dough. Divide dough into 16 equal pieces and roll into balls.

Heat oil for deep-frying to 180°C (350°F). Fry coconut balls in batches for about 5 minutes or until they are golden brown. Remove with a slotted spoon and drain on a plate lined with kitchen paper, then transfer to a large heatproof bowl.

To make the syrup, gently heat sugar and water in a pan until sugar dissolves. Bring to the boil and simmer for 1 minute. Stir in coconut flavouring. Pour hot syrup over coconut balls. Set aside to cool.

To serve, chop watermelon into chunks. Chop pineapple rings. Divide coconut balls between serving plates and drizzle with any syrup remaining in bowl. Serve coconut balls with watermelon and pineapple and scatter pomegranate seeds and grated coconut on top.

Serves 4

cinnamon beignets with blueberry sauce

see variations page 252

These crisp, golden puffs simply melt in your mouth and are deliciously addictive. Like most fritters, they are best eaten immediately.

for the sauce
450 g (1 lb) fresh blackberries
150 ml (5 fl oz) cold water
55 g (2 oz) granulated sugar
juice of 1 orange
1 tbsp arrowroot
for the beignets
110 g (4 oz) plain flour

1 tsp ground cinnamon
125 ml (4 fl oz) water
55 g (2 oz) unsalted butter, cut into pieces
2 medium eggs, beaten
finely grated rind of ½ orange
1 tbsp caster sugar
vegetable or peanut oil for deep-frying
icing sugar, to dust

To make sauce, heat blackberries in a pan with 125 ml (4 fl oz) water, sugar and orange juice. Cover and simmer for 10 minutes and set aside. Mix arrowroot with 2 tablespoons cold water and set aside. To make beignets, sieve flour and cinnamon onto a plate. Heat water and butter in a pan until melted. Bring to a fast boil, remove from heat and tip in all the flour. Beat vigorously with a wooden spoon until mixture forms a smooth ball. Cool for a few minutes, then gradually beat in eggs. Beat in orange rind and sugar. Heat oil for deep-frying to 160°C (325°F). Drop teaspoonfuls of batter into hot oil and fry beignets in batches for 4–5 minutes until puffed and golden. Remove with a slotted spoon and drain on kitchen paper. Stir arrowroot mixture until smooth and mix into sauce. Reheat sauce over low heat until thickened. Serve beignets warm with sauce and dusted with icing sugar.
Serves 4

orange crêpes with pears & grapes

see variations page 253

The pears should be ripe but still firm, as if they're too soft they'll turn mushy and start to fall apart in the sauce. Any variety of pear can be used.

for the crêpes
110 g (4 oz) plain flour
1 tbsp caster sugar
finely grated rind of 1 orange
2 large eggs
200 ml (7 fl oz) milk
75 ml (3 fl oz) water
25 g (1 oz) unsalted butter, melted, plus extra
    butter for frying

for the sauce
2 oranges
85 g (3 oz) granulated sugar
juice of 1 lemon
55 g (2 oz) unsalted butter, cut up
2 pears, peeled, cored and sliced
110 g (4 oz) seedless green grapes

To make crêpes, sieve flour into a bowl and stir in sugar and rind. Make a well in centre of the flour, add eggs and whisk. Mix milk and water and whisk into the crêpe mixture. Stir in 2 tablespoons melted butter, pour into measuring jug and set aside for 30 minutes. To cook crêpes, melt a little butter in a nonstick frying pan and pour in a little batter, swirling pan so it coats the base in a thin layer. Cook for 1–2 minutes until underside is golden and flip over to cook other side for about 30 seconds. Slide crêpe off pan onto a plate and keep warm. Cook rest of batter to make 12 crêpes. To make sauce, slice rind from 1 orange into fine strips. Set aside. Squeeze juice from both oranges and add to a pan with sugar and lemon juice. Cook until sugar dissolves, then add butter. Add pear and grapes with rind and baste with juices. Cook for 1–2 minutes until pears soften. Serve crêpes with hot fruit and juices spooned over.

Serves 6

choc 'n' nut crêpes

see variations page 254

The chocolate sauce on these crêpes makes them richer and perfect for a special treat. As with the previous crêpe recipe, these are best eaten as soon as possible after cooking.

for the crêpes
110 g (4 oz) plain flour
2 large eggs
200 ml (7 fl oz) milk
75 ml (3 fl oz) cold water
1 tbsp caster sugar
25 g (1 oz) unsalted butter, melted, plus extra
    butter for frying

for the chocolate sauce
150 g (5½ oz) milk or plain chocolate, chopped
150 ml (5½ fl oz) natural yogurt
½ tsp vanilla essence
to serve
toasted pine kernels
fresh raspberries

To make crêpes, sieve flour into a mixing bowl, make a well in the centre and add eggs. Whisk until eggs start to combine with flour. Mix the milk and water together and gradually whisk in. Add sugar and melted butter and whisk until smooth. Transfer batter to measuring jug and set aside for 30 minutes. To make chocolate sauce, melt chocolate in a bowl over a pan of hot water until smooth. Remove bowl from heat and whisk in yogurt and vanilla. Set aside. To cook crêpes, grease a nonstick frying pan with butter and pour in a little batter, swirling pan so it coats the base in a thin layer. Cook for 1–2 minutes until underside is golden and flip over to cook other side to make 12-16 crêpes. Slide crêpe off pan onto a plate and keep warm. Cook remaining mixture. Fold or roll crêpes and divide between serving plates. Drizzle with chocolate sauce and scatter with a generous amount of toasted pine kernels and fresh raspberries.

Serves 4

chocolate chip waffles

see variations page 255

The smell of these cooking will get everyone out of bed in double-quick time.

for the chocolate sauce
300 ml (10 fl. oz) double cream
225 g (8 oz) plain chocolate, broken into pieces
1 tbsp golden syrup
for the waffles
175 g (6 oz) flour
1½ tsp baking powder
2 tbsp sugar

75 g (3 oz) plain chocolate chips
½ tsp salt
300 ml (10 fl. oz) milk
2 large eggs
60 g (2½ oz) butter, melted, plus extra for cooking
icing sugar, to serve

To make the chocolate sauce, heat the cream in a medium saucepan until almost boiling. Add the chocolate and golden syrup, and stir until the chocolate has melted and the sauce is smooth and creamy. Serve hot or cold.

Preheat the waffle iron. In a large bowl, using a fork, mix together the flour, baking powder, sugar, chocolate chips and salt. In another bowl, whisk the milk and eggs together, then pour into the flour mixture. Mix together with the fork until there are no large lumps, but do not overmix. Stir in the 5 tablespoons melted butter. When the iron is hot, lightly brush it with some melted butter, then spoon in enough batter to just cover the base. Remember the batter will rise and spread during cooking. Cook for 3–5 minutes, until crisp. Keep warm while you make the rest. Serve immediately, sprinkled with a little icing sugar and with the chocolate sauce on the side.

Makes 8 waffles

variations

fruit tempura

see base recipe page 233

fruit tempura with green tea cream
Prepare basic recipe, replacing orange rind and juice with 2 tablespoons icing sugar and 1 teaspoon powdered green tea.

fruit tempura with raspberry sauce
Prepare basic recipe, serving tempura with raspberry sauce instead of orange cream. Simmer 450 grams (1 pound) raspberries with 110 grams (4 ounces) caster sugar until soft, then push through a sieve and discard seeds.

hazelnut-filled plum & apricot tempura
Prepare basic recipe, using just 6 red plums and 6 apricots. Mix together 40 grams (1½ ounces) finely chopped hazelnuts, 1 tablespoon light brown sugar and 3 tablespoons cream cheese. Halve the fruit, remove the stones and sandwich the halves back together with the hazelnut mixture.

fruit tempura with sesame seed batter
Prepare basic recipe, adding 1 tablespoon white or black sesame seeds to batter with the dry ingredients.

fruit tempura with anise seed batter
Prepare basic recipe. Add 2 teaspoons anise seeds to batter.

blueberry fritters & apricot sauce

see base recipe page 234

berry fritters with golden plum & maple sauce
Prepare basic recipe, replacing apricots in sauce with stoned yellow plums.
Instead of honey, use maple syrup, adding a little extra to taste, if necessary.

minted berry fritters with apricot sauce
Prepare basic recipe, adding 2 teaspoons chopped fresh mint to the
fritter batter.

banana and raspberry fritters with apricot sauce
Prepare basic recipe, replacing blueberries with 1 medium banana, peeled
and chopped.

spiced berry fritters with apricot sauce
Prepare basic recipe, adding 1 teaspoon mixed spice to fritter batter.

pineapple fritters with apricot sauce
Prepare basic recipe, replacing blueberries and raspberries with 3 fresh or
canned pineapple rings, blotted with kitchen paper to remove excess juice and
chopped into small pieces.

variations

chinese toffee pineapple & bananas

see base recipe page 237

chinese toffee pineapple & bananas with fennel seeds
Prepare basic recipe, greasing plate with a mild-flavoured oil such as sunflower and adding 1 tablespoon fennel seeds rather than sesame seeds to the caramel.

chinese toffee apples
Prepare basic recipe, replacing pineapple and bananas with 3 dessert apples peeled, cored and cut into 8 wedges each.

nutty chinese toffee pineapple & bananas
Prepare basic recipe, replacing sesame seeds with 3 tablespoons chopped mixed nuts.

gingered chinese toffee pineapple and bananas
Prepare basic recipe, adding 1 teaspoon ground ginger to flour when making the batter. Replace sesame seeds with finely sliced julienne strips of root ginger.

chinese toffee pears
Prepare basic recipe, replacing pineapple and bananas with 2 ripe but firm pears, peeled, cored and cut into 6 wedges each, and 1 nashi (Asian) pear, peeled, cored and cut into 8 wedges.

Thai coconut pancakes with watermelon, star fruit & pomegranate seeds

see base recipe page 238

thai coconut balls with lemongrass syrup
Prepare basic recipe. Omit coconut flavouring from syrup. Heat 1 stalk lemongrass, crushed, with sugar and water. Allow to cool before straining.

thai ginger & lime balls
Prepare basic recipe, replacing coconut milk powder with cow's milk powder and use cow's milk in dough balls. Replace coconut flavouring in syrup with 15-mm (half-inch) piece root ginger, grated and the grated rind and juice of 1 lime.

thai coconut balls with rosewater syrup
Prepare basic recipe, replacing coconut flavouring in syrup with ½ teaspoon rosewater and scattering rose petals over the fruit before serving.

thai coconut balls with orange syrup
Prepare basic recipe, replacing coconut flavouring in syrup with finely grated rind and juice of 1 orange.

thai coconut balls with star anise & cinnamon syrup
Prepare basic recipe, adding 2 whole star anise and 1 cinnamon stick, broken into 2 or 3 pieces, to sugar and water when making syrup.

variations

cinnamon beignets with blueberry sauce

see base recipe page 241

spiced beignets with blackberry sauce
Prepare basic recipe, replacing cinnamon with 1 teaspoon mixed spice.

cinnamon beignets with apricot sauce
Prepare basic recipe, serving beignets with apricot, rather than blackberry, sauce. To make sauce, simmer 175 grams (6 ounces) dried apricots with 500 ml (16 fl oz) freshly squeezed orange juice in a covered pan for 10 minutes, until apricots are soft. Purée apricots with juice, diluting with extra juice or water if necessary.

ginger beignets with blackberry sauce
Prepare basic recipe, replacing cinnamon with 1 teaspoon ground ginger.

blueberry beignets
Prepare basic recipe, stirring 110 grams (4 ounces) blueberries, dusted lightly with flour, into beignet batter. Serve cooked beignets with Greek yogurt rather than blackberry sauce.

banana beignets with blackberry sauce
Prepare basic recipe, stirring 1 small banana, peeled, chopped and dusted lightly with flour, into beignet batter.

orange crêpes with pears & grapes

see base recipe page 242

chocolate crêpes with pears & grapes
Prepare basic recipe, replacing 1 tablespoon flour with cocoa powder.

orange crêpes with lemon sauce
Prepare basic recipe, replacing oranges with 3 large lemons. Cut rind
from 1 lemon into fine strips. Squeeze juice of 3 lemons into a pan, with
110 grams (4 ounces) caster sugar. Heat to dissolve sugar, then stir in butter.

orange crêpes with strawberries & strawberry sauce
Prepare basic recipe, replacing pears and grapes with 250 grams (9 ounces)
strawberries, hulled and sliced. Replace orange sauce with strawberry sauce,
made by puréeing 250 grams (9 ounces) strawberries with 1 tablespoon
lemon juice, 2 tablespoons caster sugar and 1 tablespoon orange liqueur.

lemon crêpes with blueberries
Prepare basic recipe, replacing orange rind in crêpes with grated rind of
1 large lemon. Replace pears and grapes in sauce with 250 grams (9 ounces)
blueberries.

cinnamon orange crêpes
Prepare basic recipe, adding 1 teaspoon ground cinnamon to crêpe batter.

variations

choc 'n' nut crêpes

see base recipe page 245

strawberry & pistachio crêpes
Prepare basic recipe, replacing chocolate sauce with strawberry coulis
(page 24) and the pine kernels with chopped pistachios.

double choc 'n' nut crêpes
Prepare basic recipe for crêpes, replacing 1 teaspoon flour with cocoa.

chocolate coconut & mango crêpes
Prepare basic recipe, replacing raspberries with chopped mango and the pine
kernels with freshly grated coconut.

choc 'n' pear crepes
Prepare basic recipe for crêpes. Peel, core and chop 2 pears. Melt 55 grams
(2 ounces) unsalted butter in a pan. Stir in 2 tablespoons granulated sugar
and cook until starting to caramelise. Add pears, toss until coated with juices
and spoon over crêpes. Drizzle with chocolate sauce and sprinkle with pine
kernels. Omit raspberries.

chocolate chip waffles

see base recipe page 246

chocolate chip & banana waffles with amaretto chocolate sauce

Prepare the basic waffles, adding 1 mashed ripe banana to the wet
ingredients. Add 1 tablespoon amaretto to the sauce.

chocolate chip & peanut butter waffles with honey peanut butter syrup

Prepare the basic waffles, adding 50 grams (2ounces) peanut butter,
loosened with a little double cream, to the wet ingredients. For the syrup,
over low heat, mix 225 grams (8 ounces) honey and 125 grams (4 ounces)
peanut butter, stirring until smooth and warm.

chocolate chip & strawberry waffles with strawberry sauce

Prepare the basic waffles, adding 50g (2oz) chopped strawberries. For
the sauce, mix 1 tablespoon cornflour with 3 tablespoons sugar and
125 ml (4 fl. oz) orange juice. Over medium heat, add 450 grams (1 pound)
chopped strawberries, 2 tablespoons strawberry jam, and 1 tablespoon
golden syrup. Heat gently until boiling, stirring. Simmer for a minute or two,
or until berries have broken down and sauce is thickened.

made in minutes

If you think you've no time to prepare a proper
dessert, think again. This chapter has lots of
delicious treats that can be prepared in minutes.
Great for quick family meals and many are
impressive enough to serve at a dinner party too.

toffee, pear & amaretti sundaes

see variations page 273

A quick and easy dessert that's pure indulgence and just what you need to pick you up after a hard day. For an even faster result, use a bought toffee or butterscotch sauce or dulce de leche rather than make your own.

for the toffee sauce
100 ml (3½ oz) whipping cream
40 g (1½ oz) unsalted butter
40g (1½ oz) dark brown sugar
3 tbsp golden syrup

for the sundaes
4 scoops chocolate ice cream
4 pear halves, fresh or tinned, chopped
6 amaretti biscuits, coarsely crushed
4 scoops vanilla ice cream

To make the toffee sauce, place cream, butter, sugar and golden syrup in a pan. Heat gently until butter, sugar and syrup melt, stirring occasionally until smooth. Set aside to cool.

To assemble the sundaes, place a scoop of chocolate ice cream in the bottom of 4 sundae glasses. Drizzle with half the cooled toffee sauce. Add half the chopped pears and half the crushed amaretti. Add vanilla ice cream and remaining pears. Drizzle with remaining toffee sauce. Scatter the rest of the amaretti on top and serve.

Serves 4

sticky fruit kebabs with lemon mascarpone

see variations page 274

When the weather is warm, these fresh fruit skewers can be cooked on a barbecue. Be careful, however, not to baste them too liberally with butter and maple syrup, because any that drips into the ashes could cause the coals to flare and scorch the lovely fruit.

for the lemon mascarpone
150 g (5½ oz) mascarpone
finely grated rind of 1 lemon
for the kebabs
12 whole strawberries
2 peaches, stoned and cut into thick wedges

2 bananas, peeled and cut into 40-mm
 (1½-inch) slices
2 figs, each cut into 6 wedges
85 g (3 oz) unsalted butter, melted
4 tbsp maple syrup

To make the lemon mascarpone, stir together mascarpone and half the lemon rind. Spoon into a small bowl and sprinkle remaining rind on top. Cover with clingfilm and chill until needed.

Preheat the barbecue or a conventional grill to high heat. To make the kebabs, divide strawberries, peach wedges, banana slices and fig wedges between 8 small skewers. Place skewers side by side on a foil-lined grill rack. Brush fruit with melted butter and half of the maple syrup. Barbecue or grill for about 5 minutes, turning skewers over several times and brushing with any juices that run out. Remove from the grill, drizzle with remaining maple syrup and serve hot with the lemon mascarpone.

Serves 4

nutty chocolate banana sticks

see variations page 275

A party treat for all ages! These can be served on their own or with ice cream.

250 g (9 oz) good-quality milk chocolate,
    chopped
85 g (3 oz) chopped mixed nuts,
    lightly toasted

2 large bananas
strawberries and Cape gooseberries (physalis)
    to serve

Put chopped chocolate in a heatproof bowl and microwave on low power for about
5 minutes or until chocolate has melted. Stir until smooth.

Spread out nuts on a plate.

Peel bananas and cut into 40-cm (1½-inch) lengths. Using a fork, dip each piece of banana
into the melted chocolate until coated. Sprinkle with nuts and place on a baking tray lined
with foil or parchment paper. Push a cocktail stick into each banana piece and leave in a cool
place (not the fridge) until set.

Add a strawberry and Cape gooseberry to each cocktail stick. Serve on their own or with
ice cream.

Serves 4

snowy berries with yogurt & toasted oats

see variations page 276

For an even quicker recipe, substitute the toasted oat mixture with bought granola. Break up any large clumps by putting the cereal in a plastic bag and crushing with a rolling pin.

15 g (½ oz) unsalted butter
85 g (3 oz) rolled oats
55 g (2 oz) chopped hazelnuts
2 tbsp light brown sugar
200 ml (7 fl oz) natural Greek yogurt

2 tbsp honey
finely grated rind of 1 small orange
175 g (6 oz) fresh raspberries
175 g (6 oz) fresh blueberries
icing sugar, to dust

Melt butter in a frying pan (preferably nonstick). Add oats and hazelnuts and cook for 1-2 minutes until lightly toasted, stirring frequently. Sprinkle with the brown sugar and cook for another minute, then remove from heat and allow to cool.

Stir yogurt, honey and orange rind together. Layer raspberries, blueberries, yogurt and oat mixture in 4 dessert glasses, finishing with fruit and a light sprinkling of oats.

Chill until ready to serve. Dust with icing sugar just before serving.

Serves 4

maple-glazed pineapple & nectarines with toasted brioche

see variations page 277

You can use fresh or canned pineapple slices for this dessert but, if using tinned, look for fruit tinned in juice rather than in syrup.

55 g (2 oz) butter
6 tbsp maple syrup
juice of 1 lemon
4 pineapple slices, each cut into 4 pieces
2 large ripe nectarines, stoned and sliced

4-8 slices brioche, depending on size
4 tbsp lemon curd (page 109)
4 tbsp dark rum

Heat butter in a large frying pan over low heat. When melted, stir in maple syrup and lemon juice. Add pineapple and nectarine slices and cook gently for 5 minutes, spooning cooking juices over the fruit.

Meanwhile, lightly toast brioche slices and spread them with the lemon curd.

Pour rum over fruit and cook for 30 seconds. Place brioche on serving plates and cover with fruit and juices from the pan. Serve immediately.

Serves 4

roasted peaches with ricotta, pistachios & honey

see variations page 278

A simple dessert that's easy to make but stylish enough to serve for a special lunch or dinner party. Soft amaretti would make a good accompaniment.

4 ripe peaches, halved and stoned
55 g (2 oz) unsalted butter, melted
2 tbsp brown sugar
2 tbsp honey

2 tsp lemon juice
150 g (5½ oz) ricotta cheese
2 tbsp coarsely chopped pistachios

Preheat the oven to 220°C (425°F/gas mark 7). Place peach halves, cut sides up, side by side in a shallow roasting pan. Drizzle or brush with melted butter. Sprinkle with sugar and roast for 10 minutes.

Stir honey and lemon juice together. As soon as peaches come out of the oven, transfer them to serving plates, top each half with a spoonful of ricotta and sprinkle with pistachios. Serve drizzled with the lemon honey.

Serves 4

peach & popcorn glories

see variations page 279

You'll need to make up the gelatin a few hours ahead so it can set, but once it is firm these glamorous sundaes can be assembled in seconds. You can buy the strawberry dessert sauce, but if you have time you can make your own using the recipe on page 24.

½ package orange jelly
4 peach halves, fresh or canned
55 g (2 oz) caramel popcorn

strawberry dessert sauce
8 scoops strawberry ice cream
chocolate shapes, to decorate

Make jelly according to package instructions and pour it into a shallow container lined with clingfilm. Chill to set, then turn out, peel off cling film and chop jelly into small cubes.

Chop peaches into small dice. Spoon a little orange gelatin and some of the popcorn into 4 sundae glasses. Add some of the peaches, a little strawberry sauce and a scoop of strawberry ice cream. Add more orange jelly, peach and popcorn and finish with scoops of ice cream and strawberry sauce.

Serve at once decorated with chocolate shapes.

Serves 6

Eton mess

see variations page 280

This traditional English dessert is said to have originated during the 1930s on the playing fields of Eton College, where it was served at the picnic held at the end of May to celebrate the annual prize giving. To begin with, it was just cream and fruit. Some say the "mess" was created when a Labrador retriever sat on the picnic basket. The meringues were a later addition.

450 g (1 lb) fresh strawberries, plus extra for
   decoration
3 tbsp orange juice

4 meringue baskets or 8 small meringue shells
200 ml (7 fl oz) double cream
200 ml (7 fl oz) Greek yogurt

Hull strawberries. Reserve half of them and purée the rest with orange juice in a food processor or liquidiser.

Chop meringues into small pieces.

Whip cream until it holds its shape, then stir in the yogurt. Slice or chop reserved strawberries and fold them into cream mixture along with meringue pieces. Divide between 4 serving glasses, layering mixture with strawberry purée. Serve decorated with extra strawberries.

Serves 4

baked plums & apples with caramelised cinnamon topping

see variations page 281

As the dish needs to go into the oven as well as under the grill, choose one that you're sure is heatproof and not your best china!

350 g (12 oz) plums, halved or quartered
    and stoned
2 apples, peeled, cored and sliced or chopped
55 g (2 oz) unsalted butter, cut up
5 tbsp light brown sugar

125 ml (4 fl oz) double cream
1 x 150g (5 oz) container whole-milk apricot or
    lemon yogurt
2 tbsp fresh or dried breadcrumbs
1 tsp ground cinnamon

Preheat oven to 180°C (350°F). Spread out plums and apple slices in a shallow heatproof dish or pie dish and dot with butter. Sprinkle with 2 tablespoons brown sugar and bake for 15–20 minutes or until the fruit has softened a little but still holds its shape.

Whip cream until thickened, stir in yogurt and spoon over the fruit, spreading it in an even layer. Mix together the remaining brown sugar, breadcrumbs and cinnamon and sprinkle over the top. Slide dish under the grill for 4–5 minutes or until the sugar caramelises. Serve warm or cold.

Serves 4

toffee, pear & amaretti sundaes

see base recipe page 257

toffee, apricot & ginger sundaes
Prepare basic recipe, replacing amaretti with gingersnaps and the pears
with apricots.

toffee, pear & coffee sundaes
Prepare basic recipe, replacing chocolate ice cream with coffee ice cream and
the amaretti with chopped nuts.

chocolate, pear & amaretti sundaes
Prepare basic recipe, replacing toffee sauce with chocolate sauce (page 24).

red berries & amaretti sundaes
Prepare basic recipe, replacing pears with 225 grams (8 ounces) fresh raspberries.
Replace toffee sauce with strawberry sauce made by puréeing 225 grams
(8 ounces) fresh strawberries with 125 ml (4 fl oz) orange juice (or use a store-
bought sauce). Replace chocolate ice cream with strawberry ice cream.

variations

sticky fruit kebabs with lemon mascarpone

see base recipe page 258

sticky fruit & marshmallow kebabs
Prepare basic recipe, adding marshmallows to skewers, alternating with fruit pieces.

sticky fruit kebabs with boozy mascarpone
Prepare basic recipe, adding a splash of limoncello to lemon mascarpone.

honeyed fruit kebabs with lemon mascarpone
Prepare basic recipe, replacing maple syrup with honey.

sticky fruit kebabs with brandy cream
Prepare basic recipe, replacing lemon mascarpone with brandy cream. Whip 125 ml (4 fl oz) double cream with 2 tablespoons brandy and 1 tablespoon sugar.

variations

nutty chocolate banana sticks

see base recipe page 260

chocolate coconut banana sticks
Prepare basic recipe, replacing nuts with lightly toasted flaked coconut.

nutty chocolate strawberry sticks
Prepare basic recipe, replacing bananas with 12 large strawberries and the mixed nuts with finely chopped hazelnuts.

nutty plain chocolate banana sticks
Prepare basic recipe, replacing milk chocolate with dark chocolate.

sesame chocolate banana sticks
Prepare basic recipe, replacing chopped nuts with sesame seeds.

variations

snowy berries with yogurt & toasted oats

see base recipe page 262

snowy berries with whisky cream & oats
Prepare basic recipe, replacing yogurt with 200 ml (7 fl oz) double cream whipped until thick with 2 tablespoons whisky and 1 tablespoon icing sugar.

snowy berries with yogurt & sunflower seeds
Prepare basic recipe, replacing oats with sunflower seeds.

snowy midnight berries with yogurt & toasted oats
Prepare basic recipe, replacing raspberries with blackberries.

snowy berries with ricotta & toasted oats
Prepare basic recipe, replacing yogurt with ricotta cheese.

maple-glazed pineapple & nectarines with toasted brioche

see base recipe page 265

maple-glazed pineapple & nectarines with almonds & raisins
Prepare basic recipe, adding 2 tablespoons chopped almonds and
2 tablespoons raisins to pan with the fruit.

maple-glazed pineapple & nectarines with chocolate brioche
Prepare basic recipe, spreading brioche with chocolate hazelnut spread
rather than lemon curd.

honey-glazed pineapple & nectarines with toasted brioche
Prepare basic recipe, replacing maple syrup with 5 tablespoons honey.

maple-glazed oranges & cherries with toasted brioche
Prepare basic recipe, replacing pineapple with 2 large oranges, peeled and
sliced and the nectarines with 250 grams (9 ounces) stoned cherries.

variations

roasted peaches with ricotta, pistachios & honey

see base recipe page 266

roasted apricots with ricotta, pistachios & honey
Prepare basic recipe, replacing peaches with 8 apricots.

roasted peaches with mascarpone, pistachios & honey
Prepare basic recipe, replacing ricotta with mascarpone.

roasted plums with ricotta, pistachios & honey
Prepare basic recipe, replacing peaches with 8 large firm plums.

roasted peaches with ricotta, walnuts & maple syrup
Prepare basic recipe, replacing pistachios with walnuts and the honey with maple syrup.

peach & popcorn glories

see base recipe page 269

raspberry & popcorn glories
Prepare basic recipe, using raspberry jelly instead of orange and 175 grams (6 ounces) fresh raspberries instead of peaches.

peach, chocolate & popcorn glories
Prepare basic recipe, using chocolate ice cream instead of strawberry and chocolate sauce (page 24) instead of strawberry sauce.

peach, butterscotch & popcorn glories
Prepare basic recipe, replacing caramel popcorn with plain sweet popcorn, orange jelly with lemon and strawberry ice cream with vanilla. Replace strawberry dessert sauce with butterscotch sauce.

peach & honeycomb glories
Prepare basic recipe, replacing half the popcorn with 1 bar chocolate-covered honeycomb (such as Crunchie bar), coarsely chopped.

variations

Eton mess

see base recipe page 270

frozen Eton mess gateau
Prepare basic recipe, spooning mixture into a loaf tin or round cake tin and pressing down in an even layer. Freeze for several hours or overnight until solid. Transfer to the fridge 30–45 minutes before serving to give the dessert time to soften but not defrost.

peach & blueberry mess
Prepare basic recipe, replacing strawberries with blueberries.

peach, red berry & chocolate mess
Prepare basic recipe, replacing half the strawberries with raspberries and drizzling with chocolate sauce just before serving.

nutty Eton mess
Prepare basic recipe, folding 3 tablespoons chopped toasted almonds into whipped cream with strawberries and meringues.

variations

baked plums & apples with caramelised cinnamon topping

see base recipe page 272

baked pears & peaches with cinnamon topping
Prepare basic recipe, using 2 pears instead of apples and 350 grams (12 ounces) peaches instead of plums.

baked plums & apples with mascarpone topping
Prepare basic recipe, replacing double cream with 200 grams (7 ounces) mascarpone used straight from the container.

baked plums & apples with nutty ginger topping
Prepare basic recipe, replacing breadcrumbs with chopped mixed nuts and the cinnamon with ground ginger.

baked plums & apricots with cinnamon topping
Prepare basic recipe, replacing apples with 8 apricots, halved and stoned.

index